Complete Study Edition

Chaucer's Canterbury Tales
the Wife of Bath

| Commentary | Interlinear Text | Glossary |

edited by

SIDNEY LAMB

Associate Professor of English,
Sir George Williams University, Montreal

Cliff's Notes
INCORPORATED

LINCOLN, NEBRASKA   68501

ISBN 0-8220-1408-4

Chaucer's Canterbury Tales
the Wife of Bath

CHAUCER WAS NEVER MORE MEANINGFUL—

. . . than when read in Cliff's "Complete Study Edition." The introductory sections give you all of the background information about the author and his work necessary for reading with understanding and appreciation. The inviting three-column arrangement of the complete text offers the maximum in convenience to the reader. Each line of Chaucer's original poetry is followed by a literal translation in simple modern English. Adjacent to the text there is a running commentary that provides clear supplementary discussion. Obscure words used by Chaucer are explained directly opposite to the line in which they occur.

SIDNEY LAMB—

. . . the editor of this Chaucer "Complete Study Edition," attended Andover Academy and Columbia University.. He was graduated from McGill University, receiving the Prince of Wales Medal for Philosophy and the Moyes Travelling Fellowship. Following graduate studies in Elizabethan literature at King's College, Cambridge, from 1949 to 1952, he became a member of the English Faculty of the University of London's University of the Gold Coast in West Africa. Professor Lamb joined the faculty of Sir George Williams University, Montreal, in 1956.

Chaucer's Canterbury Tales
the Wife of Bath

Contents

An Introduction to Geoffrey Chaucer

His Life 6

His World 8

An Introduction to *The Wife of Bath*

The Prologue and Tale 10

Chaucer's Language 11

Sound 12

Versification 12

Form 13

Bibliography 14

THE WIFE OF BATH'S PROLOGUE . . . 17

THE WIFE OF BATH'S TALE 53

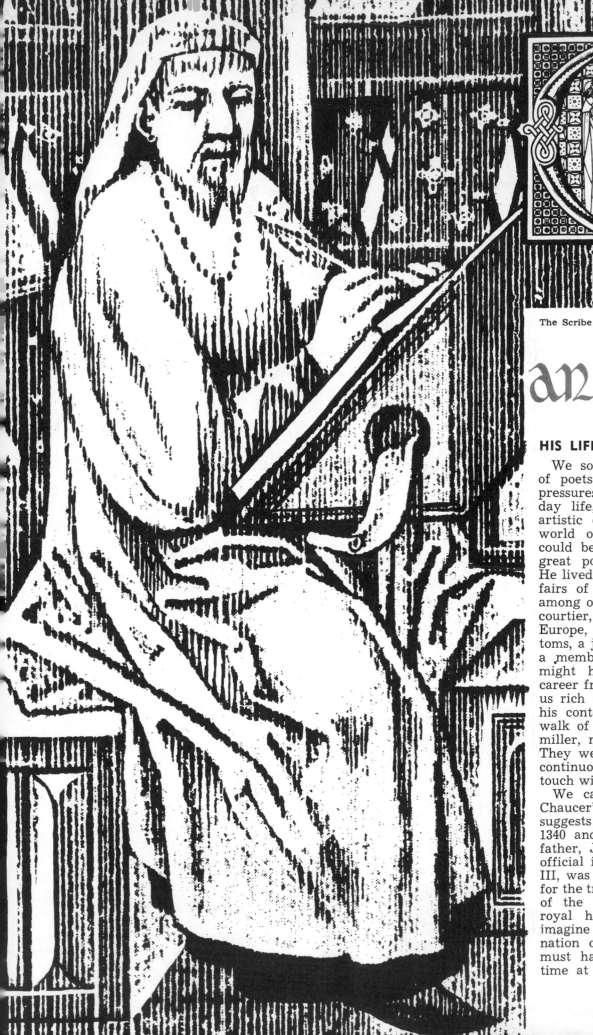

The Scribe

an introdu

HIS LIFE

We sometimes tend to think of poets as living outside the pressures and problems of everyday life, concerned only with artistic creation in a remote world of their own. Nothing could be less true of our first great poet, Geoffrey Chaucer. He lived at the center of the affairs of his day, having been, among other things, a soldier, a courtier, a royal emissary to Europe, a controller of customs, a justice of the peace and a member of parliament. We might have expected such a career from the artist who gave us rich and varied portraits of his contemporaries from every walk of life: knight, innkeeper, miller, monk, and all the rest. They were created by someone continuously and sensitively in touch with the life around him.

We cannot positively date Chaucer's birth but the evidence suggests he was born between 1340 and 1344 in London. His father, John Chaucer, a minor official in the court of Edward III, was the vintner responsible for the transmission and disposal of the wines for the various royal households. We may imagine the effect on the imagination of his young son, who must have spent much of his time at the wharves, watching

Travelers at an Inn

Studying the Word of God

...ction to Geoffrey Chaucer

the unloading of the great casks of "the wyn of Spaigne that crepeth subtilly," or the "whyte wine of Oseye [Alsace] and red wine of Gascoigne," and listening to the strange stories of the sailors from France and Spain, and the tales of the British dockhands. Chaucer's introduction to the rank and file of the society which he was later to use as his material in *The Canterbury Tales* began early. John Chaucer's position was a respectable one, and his son was awarded a position of page in a household of royal rank—that of Prince Lionel, one of the sons of Edward III. Although the exact extent of Chaucer's education is unknown, to be a page in such a household was a preparation for entrance into court society, and it was a thorough and valuable education. The young Chaucer would have been exposed to French and Latin (which were, respectively, the languages of the court and church), and he would have encountered the elegant code of manners and the elaborate ceremonies of court life.

In 1367 Chaucer was receiving a pension as a yeoman or groom in the king's household and by 1368 he is recorded as an "Esquire" in the king's retinue, which indicates a significant advancement. The court of Edward

III comprised the highest personages of the realm in political power, and in intellectual and artistic prestige. Chaucer was now in a position where he would be exposed to exalted figures and have some peripheral part in the great events of his day. It is perhaps surprising that, rising as he had from the vintner's-son-become-page to a place of prominence, that he did not lose his understanding of the common people. We know from the *Canterbury Tales* that he did not, and from some of his other writings, that he was always able to view the aristocratic environment with objectivity and something like ironic tolerance. Chaucer remained—and we may be thankful for it—primarily a poet. Whatever his involvement in the stirring business of the court, he never lost the observant, perceptive qualities of the artist.

In 1366 he married Philippa de Roet, a lady in attendance on the queen, and about this period began a series of foreign missions as the court representative. More importantly, these travels served to enlarge his experience and bring him into fruitful contact with the European literature of his day. French culture was already familiar, French still being the language of much court and diplomatic business,

and French literature widely read and admired. It was Italy that provided the most stimulating literary experience for Chaucer. Italy has always exerted an important influence on the English poets, through its vivid color and Mediterranean sunlight as much as through its poetry, and this was as true in the fourteenth century as it was to be again in the sixteenth and the nineteenth. Chaucer probably had a reading knowledge of Italian before he first went to Italy, and by the time of his second visit (in 1378) he was certainly proficient in the language. There he was to receive strong doses of Dante, Petrarch, and Boccaccio, from whom he learned and borrowed. These authors had forsaken classical Latin and French to write in their native Italian. Chaucer adopted the idea and wrote in the current Middle English. The foreign excursions are largely responsible for what critics call Chaucer's "French" and "Italian" periods, and they include some of his finest poems: *The House of Fame, The Parliament of Fowls, The Legend of Good Women,* and *Troilus and Criseyde.* But Chaucer's greatest work is reserved for his last, or "English" period.

Chaucer was by this time an important official: in 1382 he be-

Various Paraphernalia from the 14th to 15th Century Period

came controller of petty customs, in 1385 justice of the peace for the county of Kent, and in 1386 a knight of the shire (member of parliament). Suddenly, through some complex shifts of power in the court, he was deprived of all his offices. He regained favor later, but we may be thankful for this political setback of 1386, since it gave Chaucer the leisure he needed. Having digested and assimilated the literature of France and Italy, the "English" period now begins with the composition of *The Canterbury Tales*. We may, by the same token, regret Chaucer's return to public service, since he was never able to finish them. He died in October 1400 and was buried in Westminster Abbey. An impressive tomb was erected over his grave in the fifteenth century, and this section of the Abbey became the burial place for the great English writers to follow Chaucer, and is called Poets' Corner. There could be no more fitting place for the grave of the Father of English Poetry.

HIS WORLD

The technological differences between our age and Chaucer's are obvious enough when we think of the weird astrological-medical theories of the "Doctour of Phisik" (*Prologue* 411-44), or of the fact that it took Chaucer's pilgrims three days of hard travel to traverse the sixty miles between London and Canterbury. The differences in society and its assumptions are impor-

tant in understanding the actions and attitudes of Chaucer's pilgrims.

The social structure of England (and all Europe) in the fourteenth century was feudal, that is to say power radiated from the king, through his nobles (when he could control them), and through their subjects, with little kingly power reaching the lower echelons of society. The king and his nobles owned the land, which was divided into great agricultural estates, and these provided the men, material, and money which supported the crown and its wars. Society was organized in a hierarchical form, one's wealth and power being a matter of what position one occupied on the hierarchical ladder. This ladder extended from the king, through the great noblemen-landlords (like Chaucer's patron, John of Gaunt, Duke of Lancaster), down through lesser landlords and their various executive officers with, at the bottom, the serfs who worked the land for their masters. It is perhaps important to note that while we may regard this system as unjust and oppressive, the medieval people could conceive of no other. Each level of society had its rights and privileges, and each had its duties and obligations. Despite the occasional abuse they regarded the system as right and proper.

Three groups of Chaucer's pilgrims may be isolated to suggest how this system worked. The

first represents agricultural feudalism (the first and basic kind) founded on land ownership and service. The Knight, who is highest on the scale, is a landowner, and has therefore served in the wars for his king, and he will be followed in this by his son, the Squire. The Knight's Yeoman is a servant, whose only duty is to the Knight. The Franklin also holds land, perhaps "in fee" from some noble, but more probably in his own right. His service is the direction of his farm, his obligation to the noble or king being doubtless in the form of the yearly harvest, and of men in time of need. The Miller does not himself own land but has been given the right to mill all grain on an estate; the Reeve manages an estate. They are both servants, but of an exalted kind, and make shrewd and profitable use of their power, as we shall see. The lowest in the hierarchy is the Plowman, who simply tills the land.

England was changing in the fourteenth century, and one of the most important changes was the growth of a new, urban society (mainly in London) where the feudal structure was somewhat modified. Neither the Doctor nor the Sergeant of the Law owned land, although they were both men of substance. The Doctor (Chaucer tells us) made money out of the plague, and the Lawyer made money out of almost everything. They were the beginning of a new class, today

Virgin and Child

called professional men. The Manciple and the Merchant and even the Wife of Bath (who is a clothmaker) also represent the urbanization process. They were not directly commanded by anyone, and in time they became the mercantile middle class who overthrew the monarchy and the last vestiges of feudalism in the civil war of the seventeenth century. It is also significant that the Haberdasher, the Carpenter, the Weaver, and the Dyer are presented together, in that they are all members of one of the great parish guilds. It was through these craft and parish guild associations that the new urban artisans achieved the power that they lacked through not belonging to the land-hierarchy.

There is yet a third group, constituting a kind of feudal system of its own, and representing one of the most powerful elements of medieval society— the church. Nine of Chaucer's thirty pilgrims belong to the clergy, and it would be difficult to overestimate the importance of the Roman Catholic church to the lives of the people of western Europe in the fourteenth century. They might disregard its teaching (as some of the pilgrims do) or complain of its abuses (as Chaucer does) but from baptism, through confirmation and marriage, to the funeral rites, it was intimately connected with their lives. It was a visibly potent force throughout England, from the great cathedrals—such

as Canterbury—and the religious houses, down to the humble parish churches.

Despite the worldly aspects of life that so often appear in *The Canterbury Tales* we should not forget that the people Chaucer gathers together are pilgrims, and that the occasion for their gathering is the spring pilgrimage to the shrine of "the holy blisfil martir," St. Thomas Becket, at Canterbury. We can gauge the importance of the church in men's lives by noting how many varieties of belief or simulated belief Chaucer presents. They run all the way from the dedicated holiness of the Parson, through the superficial observances of the Prioress, to the outright hypocrisy of the Summoner and Pardoner. Chaucer, looking about him, sees fit to define a large proportion of his characters by where they stand with regard to the church.

It is sometimes suggested that the medieval world was a happier, simpler, and less troubled time than our own. In some ways this is true—certainly Chaucer's pilgrims are free from many of our modern anxieties— yet the fourteenth century had its own troubles, and it is an oversimplification to regard it as a time of innocent good humor. In fact it is the overall good humor of Chaucer's treatment that has fostered this view, and while he is basically optimistic, he would be unlikely to accept it.

The plague, or Black Death (to

which Chaucer occasionally alludes) entered England in midcentury with dreadful consequences. It is said that half the population was wiped out, and while this may be an exaggeration, it is no exaggeration to say that medieval man lived in constant fear of its ravages. One of the effects of the plague was to inflate prices and further depress the already grim living conditions of those at the bottom of the economic ladder. This in turn produced the insurrection known as the Peasants' Revolt (1381), in which the infuriated mob murdered a good many of those whom they regarded as their exploiters. Chaucer—as a justice of the peace and a member of parliament—might be expected to be bitter about this unprecedented attack on the social order. It may be a measure of his magnanimity that only a few years after the rebellion his portrait of the Plowman in the *Prologue* is remarkable for its praise of the peasant virtues.

The Hundred Years War continued, with the French threatening to invade England; this is one of the reasons for the warlike nature of Chaucer's Shipman, whose merchant ship was obliged to be a fighting vessel, and it also accounts for the Merchant's anxiety about trade if the shipping route between Middleburg in the Netherlands and Orwell in England is broken.

The church itself was divided at the time, one faction having a pope at Rome and the other at Avignon, with some of Europe (including England) supporting the first and some (including Scotland) the second. The confusion resulting from this situation was probably in part the cause of the clerical abuses that produced so much complaint (some of it in the *Canterbury Tales*) during the period.

If we set these disruptions alongside the achievements of art and literature, the security of a stable society, and the calm that comes from faith (the qualities usually presented as typical of the Middle Ages), we shall probably be somewhere near the truth. At any rate it was a time of transition and great variety: an appropriate time for the creation of a work as varied and multicolored as *The Canterbury Tales*.

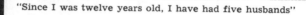

"Since I was twelve years old, I have had five husbands"

an introduction to

THE PROLOGUE AND TALE

Of all the pilgrims who embarked on the memorable journey to Canterbury, none has evoked more comment than the Wife of Bath. A recent editor of the *Canterbury Tales* has called her "Chaucer's most wonderful creation," and the great Chaucerian scholar G. L. Kittredge has gone so far as to say that the Wife is "one of the most amazing characters that the brain of man has ever conceived." We get a vivid sketch of her in the *General Prologue*. Chaucer makes much of her lavish dress: her headdresses are so heavy that "they weyeden ten pound," her hose are "of fyn scarlet reed," and she herself has a face "boold and fair and reed of hue." She comes into her own when called upon to deliver her tale. Her prologue alone is as long as the whole of the *General Prologue*. One of her outstanding qualities is her talkativeness. She can never get through a piece of narration without a series of asides, illustrations, remembered incidents, and all the rest of the conversational overflow so typical of modern, as well as medieval, ladies when they have something they feel needs to be said.

The Wife is most fully revealed in her prologue, which is a long, rambling account of her

five marriages, sometimes vulgar, sometimes spiteful, sometimes hilarious, sometimes sad, but always interesting. It leaves an overall impression of a woman who has lived her life as fully as possible, without regret, and with an insatiable appetite for the pleasures life has to offer. In an age in which literature exalted idealism and otherworldliness, she is happily and frankly committed to this world, and where the clerics on the journey to Canterbury argue for spirituality (often hypocritically) she argues for the delights of the senses. Five husbands are not enough — "Welcome the sixte whan that evere he shal!"

All the commentators on the Wife agree on her vigorous and ebullient character, but not many notice the subtle qualifications Chaucer has given it. Although she seems to be the life-force incarnate, she is afraid of aging and death:

But age, allas, that al wol envenyme,
Hath me biraft my beautee and my pith. . . .

But no sooner does she voice this realization of aging than she reacts against it, with typical energy: "Lat go, farewel, the devel go therwith!" Although she is as material-minded as any (see her treatment of her first three husbands) yet, when the time

"God bade us expressly to increase and multiply"

Wed at the church door

the Wife of Bath

comes to tell her tale, she presents a combination of fairy folk-lore and chivalric morality and mysticism. Her language is as coarse and earthy as any in the *Canterbury Tales*, yet she swears continually "by God," and Chaucer gives us no reason to think of her as a hypocrite. Chaucer allows us to see the one thing about the Wife that she herself, for all her hardheaded realism, cannot see: her oncoming age. She is contemptuous of the cleric who, "in his dotage," sits down to write about and condemn "Venus werkes." Yet she herself is past her prime, as she half admits in the moving lines that begin at 469 — "But Lord Crist! whan that it remembereth me/ Upon my youthe and on my joli-tee." It is this half-conscious recognition of the passage of time that gives point to her choice of a tale.

There has been a good deal of scholarly debate about the Wife's tale, the general opinion being that Chaucer first wrote what is now the Shipman's tale for her and later, on maturer considera-tion, gave it to the Shipman and wrote another tale for the Wife. The Shipman's tale has passages such as this:

The sely housbonde, algate he moote paye,
He moot us clothe, and he moot us arraye,
Al for his owene worshipe richely,

In which array we daunce jolily. . . .

which could hardly come from that rough, piratical character (whom we cannot imagine talk-ing about how his wife must clothe him) and which must originally have been written for the Wife. The second, and final, tale which Chaucer composed for the Wife fits in to a pattern that must have emerged during his work on the *Canterbury Tales*. Some of these tales fall into what Kittredge has called the "mar-riage group" — they are about, and take different attitudes to, the woes and joys of marriage. As he developed this theme, Chaucer no doubt saw that the Wife of Bath ought to be central to it and wrote the present tale as her contribution to the debate about whether the husband or the wife ought to have "sover-aynetee" in marriage. It is a long debate, including many points of view. In the Clerk's tale, for ex-ample, marital virtue is exempli-fied by the long-suffering "pa-tient Griselda." In the Mer-chant's tale, wifely treachery seems recommended. In the Franklin's tale of Dorigen and Arveragus marriage is founded on mutual trust, whereas in the Nun's Priest's tale the husband comes to grief just because he trusts his wife. The Wife of Bath, in both her prologue and

her tale, is dedicated to the notion that the wife's "soveraynetee" is what makes marriage work-able. It is characteristic that she does not use logic to establish her point, for example: her fifth hus-band is only happy after she dumps him into the fireplace and makes him yield all material au-thority to her. In her tale the knight achieves his happiness by yielding to his "loathly" aged wife, thereby restoring her youth and beauty.

It is the Wife, and not her les-son, that we remember. In his choice of a tale for her Chaucer has subtly implied her resent-ment at growing old and losing the delights of the senses. How-ever coarse and vulgar we may find her, she is committed to life and all its pleasures. Many critics have suggested that her statement concerning her "youthe" and "jolitee" is also Chaucer's, as he looks back on a long and full life:

But Lord Crist! whan that it remembreth me
Upon my youthe and on my jolitee,
It tikleth me aboute myn herte roote;
Unto this day it dooth myn herte boote
That I have had my world as in my tyme.

CHAUCER'S LANGUAGE

The Canterbury Tales were written nearly six hundred years ago, and the English language

"The first three men were good, rich, and old. So help me God, I laugh when I remember that they gave me their land and wealth."

has changed a good deal in that time. It has not changed so much, however, that the reader who is prepared to spend a little time cannot recover much of the full flavor of Chaucer's language. With a little study and practice one will find himself at home with Chaucer's sounds and meanings and will derive real pleasure from becoming familiar with Chaucerian turns of phrase and tartness of expression.

This edition of the *Wife of Bath's Prologue and Tale* provides both an interlinear translation and a glossary, so there should be no trouble in understanding what Chaucer is saying. However, one point about the change of word meanings between the fourteenth and twentieth centuries ought to be made. The difficulty with a word may arise because the word is completely unknown to us: it has simply dropped out of the language (e.g., *bismotered* for "stained") and here the reader need only look at the translation or glossary.

A different sort of difficulty arises when we come across a word in Chaucer that we still use, but with a quite different sense. For example, when we read that the Friar is "a ful solempne man," we may understand *solempne* to be our "solemn" (which is has become), but this seems hardly the word to apply to the gay Friar. We have lost the word's original meaning —"festive"—which it takes straight over from the Latin. There are a good many words

like this in Chaucer, where what seems to us the obvious, that is, modern, meaning is not the Chaucerian meaning, and the reader has to watch for them.

SOUND

Scholars have been able to reconstruct the approximate sounds of Chaucer's language. Since he was a poet who meant his work to be read aloud, we ought to be able to hear, if only with the ear of the imagination, how his lines sounded. For an extensive list of the phonetic differences between current pronunciation and that of the fourteenth century, consult either the Robinson or Baugh edition given in the bibliography. However, there are three rules that will give a reasonable rendition of Chaucerian spoken English.

1. Pronounce all written consonants as we do in modern English. However, *gh* as in *night*, though now silent, was pronounced like the *ch* in the Scottish *loch* or the German *Bach*.

2. Pronounce all the syllables in a word, even the final *-e*, which is unstressed at present. Chaucer's *dame* was pronounced *dah-meh*, and *dames* was *dah-mess*. However, the stress on such final syllables is light.

3. Pronounce all written vowels in the way in which they would be pronounced in modern French or Italian. Thus Chaucer's *page* has an *a* pronounced *ah*, like the *a* in the French *plage*, so *page* is pronounced *pahj-eh*. Chaucer's *fame* is *fah-meh*, *name* is *nah-meh*.

Pronounce the vowel spelled *e* or *ee* in Chaucer's *regioun* as the *ay* sound of modern French *région* (or modern English *rate*), not as the *ee* sound of the modern English *region*. There are exceptions to this, but the main point is that Chaucer's *e* is never pronounced as the *ee* sound of the modern English *region, me,* and so on.

Pronounce the vowel spelled *i* or *y* in Chaucer's *fine* as the *ee* sound in modern French *fine* (or English *machine*), not as the *eye* sound in modern English *fine*. Other examples are *bite, glide, kynde, prime, ride, strive,* and so on.

Pronounce the vowel spelled *ou* or *ow* in Chaucer's *doute* as the *ou* sound in modern French *doute* (or modern English *soup*), not as the *ow* sound in modern English *doubt*. Other examples are *foul, hous,* and *mous*.

VERSIFICATION

Much more important than phonetic correctness in Chaucer is understanding the metrical structure of his lines, and fortunately this is fairly simple. In most of *The Canterbury Tales* (and in the *General Prologue*) Chaucer used the rhymed iambic pentameter, or five-beat couplet, later to become famous (with Dryden and Pope) as the heroic couplet. The important thing here is to discover, by experimental reading, the way in which the five beats fall in the line. The experimental element lies in discovering the changed accent in some words, and in others

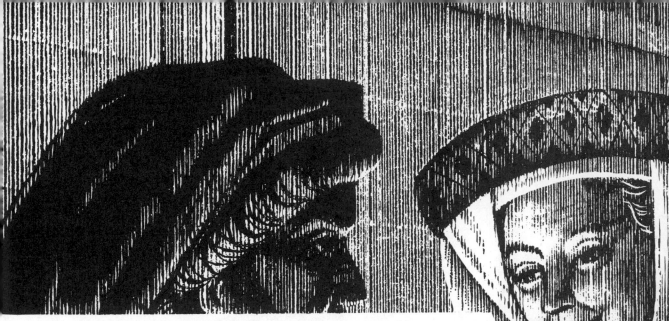

"Welcome the sixth, whenever he comes along"

whether or not the final -e is to be sounded. As an example of the first, take the line

He hadde maad ful many a mariage.

We are tempted to say

He had made full many a marriage,

which spoils Chaucer's five-beat rhythm. But if we sound the final -e in hadde, and take notice of the unfamiliar accent in mariage, the line will read, correctly,

He hádd-e maád ful mány a máriage.

In the line

She hadde passed many a straunge strem,

we are tempted to say,

She had passed many a strange stream.

The failure to sound the final -e that we either no longer have or no longer sound makes this metrically incorrect. The metrically correct version is

She hádd-e páss-ed mány a stráung-e strém.

After a little reading of Chaucer's iambic pentameter the reader begins to distinguish easily between the mute and the sounded final -e.

FORM

Some of Chaucer's grammatical forms and constructions are strange to us. There are a good many, but here are some of the more frequent differences between Middle and Modern English:

Most verb forms resemble their modern counterparts, but the following peculiarities should be noted. Chaucer normally uses the form (he, she, it) loveth rather than the modern verb form loves. Verbs with stems ending in -d, or -t, however, regularly contract the ending -eth, thus appearing as he bit (for biddeth), fint (findeth), holt (holdeth), stant (standeth).

Many verb endings had a final -n, now gone, which might be dropped. Thus we (ye, they) love and loven are used interchangeably for modern we love; we lovede(n) for modern we loved; and to love(n) for modern to love. Also optional was prefix y as a sign of the past participle, so that modern I have loved appears sometimes as I have y-loved, and I have drunk as I have y-dronke(n).

One sign of the negative was the still familiar not or its variants noght and naught. Another sign, now gone, was ne or n', which was often accompanied by other negative words. "He nevere yet no vileynye ne sayde/ In al his lyf unto no maner wight" means literally, "He never yet no villainy didn't say to no kind of person," that is, he never yet spoke any villainy to any kind of person. Ne combines with the word that follows in the frequently occurring collocations nadde (ne hadde, "hadn't"), nere ("weren't"), nolde ("wouldn't"), noot (ne woot, "know not"), nyl ("will not"), nyste (ne wiste, "knew not").

13

Bibliography

EDITIONS

Baugh, A. C., ed. *Chaucer's Major Poetry.* Appleton-Century-Crofts, 1963. Contains all the *Canterbury Tales* as well as the rest of Chaucer's most important poems. Notes and glossary are excellent.

Manly, J. M., and E. Rickert, eds. *The Text of the Canterbury Tales.* 8 vols., Chicago University Press, 1940. The definitive modern edition, with variant readings, and extended notes and glossary.

Robinson, F. N., ed. *The Works of Geoffrey Chaucer,* Houghton Mifflin, 1957. The best one-volume edition of the complete works, with full introductions and notes to the individual poems.

COMMENTARY AND CRITICISM

Bennett, H. S. *Chaucer and the Fifteenth Century.* Oxford University Press, 1947. A thoroughgoing treatment of the literary and social background.

Bowden, Muriel A. *Commentary on the General Prologue to the Canterbury Tales.* Macmillan, 1948. Extensive background material on the characters who appear in *The Prologue.*

Chute, Marchette. *Goeffrey Chaucer of England.* Dutton, 1946. A popular account of Chaucer's life.

Coghill, Nevill. *The Poet Chaucer.* Oxford University Press, 1949. Scholarly and authoritative treatment of poet's career.

French, R. D. *Chaucer Handbook.* Appleton-Century-Crofts, 1947. Useful notes on each of Chaucer's works with the emphasis on factual detail rather than critical evaluation.

Lowes, J. L. *Geoffrey Chaucer.* Indiana University Press, 1958. A very perceptive critical analysis.

Trevelyan, G. M. *Illustrated English Social History, I: Chaucer's England and the Early Tudors.* Longmans, 1949. A valuable study of Chaucer's social and cultural background.

The Wife of Bath

The Wife of Bath's Prologue

The Prologe of the Wyves Tale of Bathe.
The Prologue of the Wife of Bath's Tale

It is quite in character that the Wife of Bath's Prologue, or "pre-amble" as she calls it, should be twice as long as the story she has to tell. The preliminary sketch of her in the General Prologue to the Canterbury Tales suggests a gregarious and garrulous woman, so her digressions, exemplary stories, and other conversational meanderings come as no surprise.

Chaucer underlines her undisciplined delivery by having her interrupt herself with continual asides ("But tel me this . . ."), rhetorical questions ("What sestow?" and "wostow why?"), and finally making her lose the thread of her narrative altogether:

"But now sire—lat me see, what shal I seyn?
Aha, by God, I have my tale ageyn. . . ."

Chaucer is particularly adept at making his pilgrims' verbal style reflect their personalities, and the Wife's style is exactly suited to her vigorous, careless, carefree attitude toward life. However, there is a pattern beneath this apparent confusion. The Wife's topic is marriage, and what she has to say about it may be divided into fairly distinct parts: multiple marriage ("Of bigamye or of octogamye"), 1-58; virginity and marriage, 59-62; and her own treatment of her five husbands, which takes up most of the remaining prologue.

"Experience, though noon auctoritee   1
"Experience, even if no other authority

Were in this world, is right ynogh for me
Were in this world, would be good enough for me

To speke of wo that is in mariage;
To speak of the woe that is in marriage;

For lordynges, sith I twelf yeer was of age—
For masters, since I was twelve years old—

Thonked be God that is eterne on lyve—   5
Thanks be to God who lives eternally—

Housbondes at chirche dore I have had fyve
I have had five husbands at church door

(If I so ofte myghte han wedded be),
(For so often have I been wedded),

And alle were worthy men in hir degree.
And all were worthy men in their degree.

But me was told, certeyn, nat longe agon is,
But certainly I have been told, not long ago,

That sith that Crist ne wente nevere but ones   10
That since Christ only went once

To weddyng in the Cane of Galilee,
To a wedding in Cana of Galilee,

That by the same ensample taughte he me
That by the same example he taught me

That I ne sholde wedded be but ones.
That I should be wedded only once.

Herke eek, lo, which a sharp word for the nones,
Hark then, what sharp words to this purpose,

Biside a welle, Jhesus, God and man,   15
Beside a well, Jesus, God and man,

Spak in repreeve of the Samaritan:
Spoke in reproof of the Samaritan:

'Thou hast yhad fyve housbondes,' quod he,
'You have had five husbands,' said he,

'And that ilke man that now hath thee
'And this man that now has you

Is nat thyn housbonde.' Thus seyde he certeyn.
Is not your husband.' Certainly he said this.

What that he mente therby I kan nat seyn;   20
What he meant by it, I cannot say;

But that I axe why that the fifthe man
But I do ask why that fifth man

The Wife of Bath

6. "at chirche dore": In the Middle Ages the marriage ceremony was performed at the door of the church, after which the assembly went inside for the Mass.

11. St. John 2:1-11. This also appears in the Epistle against Jovinian, by Jerome, from which the Wife takes other examples and arguments. See Commentary.

16. The dialogue between Christ and the woman of Samaria appears in St. John 4:6-26.

THE WIFE OF BATH

[Lines 22-44a]

Although the Wife of Bath is an intensely individual creation, in composing her portrait Chaucer has drawn on various literary sources, two of which are of special interest.

The first of these is a long French poem of the thirteenth century called Le Roman de la Rose. The first part of the poem, by Guillaume de Lorris, is an allegory representing a romantic, idealized form of love very common in the literature of the Middle Ages (and which will be discussed later in this commentary). The second part, by Jean de Meun, is quite different. In it love is treated in a satirical and even cynical fashion, as a physical appetite rather than a spiritual ideal.

It is of interest to note that early in his career Chaucer translated the first part of the Roman, but that later, in the writing of the Canterbury Tales, he draws heavily on the second part, especially in his portrait of the Wife. Here, for example, is La Vieille, a disillusioned old woman in the Roman, recalling her dealings with her lovers:

"When I had wit through practice won,
A thing with no small labour done,
Full many a noble man did I
Trick and beguile most skilfully.
. . ."

We might almost be listening to the Wife recounting her victories over her first three husbands. Chaucer has taken de Meun's harsh realism and made it an element in the Wife's frankly material, physical view of love and marriage; but there is, of course, much more in her character than this.

The second notable source for the Wife's prologue is a document written by St. Jerome in the fourth century, called the Epistle against Jovinian. Jovinian was a monk who had written a pamphlet attacking the asceticism of the church and denying that chastity

Was noon housbonde to the Samaritan?
Was not a husband to the Samaritan?

How manye myghte she have in mariage?
How many could she have in marriage?

Yet herde I nevere tellen in myn age
Yet I have never heard in all my life

Upon this nombre diffinicioun.   25
An explanation of this number.

Men may devyne and glosen up and doun,
Men may guess and explain up and down,

But wel I woot, expres, withouten lye,
But well I know, expressly, without lying .

God bad us for to wexe and multiplye;
God told us to increase and multiply;

That gentil text kan I wel understonde.
That noble text I can quite understand.

Eek wel I woot he seyde myn housbonde   30
And also I know well he said my husband

Sholde lete fader and moder and take to me;
Should leave father and mother and take me;

But of no nombre mencion made he
But he made no mention of number

Of bigamye or of octogamye;
Of bigamy or of octogamy;

Why sholde men thanne speke of it vileynye?
Why should men speak evil of it?

  Lo, here the wise kyng, daun Salomon;   35
  Consider here the wise king, Lord Solomon;

I trowe he hadde wyves mo than oon.
I believe he had more wives than one.

As wolde God it leveful were to me
Would God it were allowed to me

To be refresshed half so ofte as he!
To be refreshed half so often as he!

Which yifte of God hadde he for alle hise wyves!
What a gift of God he had with all his wives!

No man hath swich that in this world alyve is.   40
No man has such such that lives in this world.

God woot this noble king, as to my wit,
God knows this noble king, as I think,

The firste nyght hadde many a murye fit
The first night had many a merry bout

With ech of hem, so wel was hym on lyve.
With each of them, so well was he able to live.

Blessed be God that I have wedded fyve,
Blessed be God that I have wedded five,

Of whiche I have pyked out the beste,   44a
Of which I have picked out the best,

King Solomon
28. The reference is to Genesis 1:28.

33. According to canon law bigamy was applied to successive marriages. Octagomy or marriage with eight husbands, is mentioned in the Epistle against Jovinian.

35. Solomon had seven hundred wives and three hundred concubines (I Kings 11:3).

44 a-f. The line numbering here is explained by the fact that in some

THE WIFE OF BATH ✓

[Lines 44b-63]

was in itself a virtue. This called forth Jerome's counterattack, which became one of the best known medieval denunciations of worldly, sensual pleasure, and supports chastity against the "evil" of marriage.

Chaucer allows the Wife to quote, or cite, Jerome's Epistle at several points (for example, in her distinction between wheat and barley bread, 143-44), and of course all these references are ironic in their effect, since the Wife's position is diametrically opposed to Jerome's.

"The Devil," St. Jerome might have said, with Shakespeare, "can cite scripture for his purpose." Chaucer, of course, remains neutral, although we may suspect his sympathies lie with the Wife's wholehearted acceptance of what the physical world has to offer.

These two sources suggest that the Wife's prologue is more than just a vivid picture of a vivid, if somewhat amoral woman. It has to be viewed also as part of the long medieval debate (of which de Meun's and Jerome's work are also a part) about the nature and morality of sexual love and the place of the woman in marriage. The Wife takes the first point first, in her discussion of virginity, and goes on to the second when she recalls in rich and often lurid detail her own marital history.

Chaucer makes no attempt to present his Wife as an unprejudiced commentator on the subject of marriage. In her very first example, Christ's reproof of the much-married Samaritan, he indicates her bias and, indeed, her lack of knowledge.

In medieval church doctrine, the marriage of man and woman was a sacrament and a kind of replica of Christ's marriage to the church. Just as Christ's relation to the church was divine and eternal, so marriage could not, or ought not to, be dissolved. For any medieval reader with any theological knowledge (much more common then than now), this would be the meaning of Christ's statement at 18.

But of this spiritual dimension the Wife is totally ignorant: "What that he mente therby I

Bothe of here nether purs and of here cheste.   44b
For under-purse as well as money-chest.

Diverse scoles maken parfyt clerkes,   44c
Different schools make perfect scholars,

And diverse practyk in many sondry werkes   44d
And different methods in many kinds of work

Maken the werkman parfit sekirly: 44e
Certainly make the workman perfect:

Of fyve husbondes scoleying am I.   44f
I have studied five husbands.

Welcome the sixte whan that evere he shal!   45
Welcome to the sixth, whenever he is ready!

For sith I wol nat kepe me chaast in al,
Indeed I shall not remain chaste forever,

Whan myn housbonde is fro the world ygon,
When my husband is gone from the world,

Som Cristen man shal wedde me anon;
Some Christian man shall wed me soon;

For thanne, th' apostle seith that I am free
For then the apostle says that I am free

To wedde, a Goddes half, where it liketh me.   50
To wed, in God's name, whomever I like.

He seith that to be wedded is no synne;
He says that to be married is no sin;

Bet is to be wedded than to brynne.
It is better to be married than to burn.

What rekketh me thogh folk seye vileynye
What do I care though folk speak evil

Of shrewed Lameth and his bigamye?
Of wicked Lamech and his bigamy?

I woot wel Abraham was an holy man,   55
I know well Abraham was a holy man,

And Jacob eek, as fer as evere I kan,
And Jacob too, as far as I know,

And ech of hem hadde wyves mo than two,
And each of them had more than two wives,

And many another holy man also.
And many another holy man as well.

Where kan ye seye in any manere age
And where can you say in any sort of age

That hye God defended mariage   60
That high God forbade marriage

By expres word? I pray you, telleth me!
By express word? I pray you, tell me!

Or where comanded he virginitee?
Or where did he command virginity?

I woot as wel as ye, it is no drede,
I know as well as you, no fear,

19

---

earlier editions these lines were omitted as being not by Chaucer; but they are genuine, and in editions in which they are restored they are numbered in this way.

49. St. Paul, in I Corinthians 7:3.

54. Lameth, Genesis 4:19, is the first man mentioned in the Bible as having two wives.

"Christ, who is the source of perfection"

THE WIFE OF BATH

[Lines 64-86]

kan nat seyn." She can and does quote copiously from the Bible and the "auctoritees" of the church, but with no real understanding. Her understanding lies in other directions, and Chaucer is careful to suggest this at the outset.

Th' apostle, whan he speketh of maydenhede,
The apostle, when he speaks of maidenhood,

He seyde that precept therof hadde he noon.　65
Says that he has no precept for it.

Men may conseille a womman to be oon,
Men may counsel a woman to be single,

But conseillyng is no comandement.
But counseling is not commandment.

He put it in oure owene juggement.
He left it to our own judgment.

For hadde God comanded maydenhede,
For had God commanded maidenhood,

Thanne hadde he dampned weddyng with the dede;　70
He would have damned wedding at the same time;

And certes, if ther were no seed ysowe,
And certainly, if no seed were sown,

Virginitee, thanne wherof sholde it growe?
Where would virgins be grown?

Poul dorste nat comanden at the leeste
Paul dared not command, at least,

A thyng of which his maister yaf noon heeste.
*Something concerning which his master gave no
　　　command.*

The dart is set up for virginitee:　75
The prize is set up for virginity:

Cacche whoso may, who renneth best lat see.
Win it who can, let us see who runs best.

　But this word is nat take of every wight,
　But this word is not intended for everyone,

But ther as God list yeve it of his myght.
But only there where it pleases God to apply it.

I woot wel that th' apostle was a mayde;
I know well that the apostle was a virgin;

But natheless, thogh that he wroot and sayde　80
But nevertheless, though he wrote and said

He wolde that every wight were swich as he,
That he would that everyone were such as he,

Al nys but conseil to virginitee;
All this only recommends virginity;

And for to been a wyf he yaf me leve
And he gave me leave to be a wife

Of indulgence; so is it no repreve
By permission; so there is no blame

To wedde me if that my make dye,　85
If I wed when my mate dies,

Withoute excepcion of bigamye;
Without the risk of bigamy;

65. "precept": i.e., from Jesus, see I Corinthians 7:6.

75. "The dart": a medieval prize for winning a race.

The Wife's first target in her campaign against the view represented by Jerome's Epistle is the belief that God commanded virginity, and her first argument is her most powerful one:

"And certes, if ther were no seed ysowe,
Virginitee, thanne wherof sholde it growe?"

She goes on to distinguish between the "conseillyng," or recommendation, to be virgin and the "comandement" to be so. At about this point we begin to get further little touches that fill out the portrait of the Wife.

St. Paul himself, foremost among the ascetics, is rallied to her cause; since he had not demanded chastity of all, "And for to been a wyf he yaf me leve." Anyone who is not against her is for her, and indeed some of those who are against her can, with some twisting, be shown to be for her. Her interest, Chaucer makes clear, is in winning an argument, not in discovering the truth.

THE WIFE OF BATH

[Lines 87-110]

Furthermore, her attitude toward virginity becomes increasingly clear as she warms to her subject. At first she seems to endorse St. Paul in the view that marriage is a necessary evil ("Bet it is to be wedded than to brynne") and to grant the superiority of virginity —the prize "is set up for virginitee."

But to this she immediately and significantly adds "cacche whoso may," and goes on to make it quite clear that this is not a prize she cares to compete for. She will "make no boast" of her condition and very soon comes to the point where she states it with something close to pride:

"He [Christ] spake to hem that wolde lyve parfitly— And lordynges, by youre leve, that am nat I!"

Pilgrims' Tokens

Al were it good no womman for to touche—
All in all it would be good to touch no woman,

He mente as in his bed or in his couche,
He meant as in his bed or on his couch,

For peril is bothe fyr and tow t' assemble;
For it is dangerous to bring fire and tow together;

Ye knowe what this ensample may resemble.   90
You know how to apply this example.

This al and som, he heeld virginitee
The sum of it is, he held virginity

Moore parfit than weddyng in freletee.
More perfect than the frailty of marriage.

(Freletee clepe I but if that he and she
(Frailty I call it, unless he and she

Wolde leden al hir lyf in chastitee.)
Were to live all their lives in chastity).

I graunte it wel, I have noon envye,   95
I grant it freely, I have no envy,

Thogh maydenhede preferre bigamye;
Though maidenhood be preferred to bigamy;

It liketh hem to be clene body and goost.
Some like purity of body and spirit.

Of myn estaat I nyl nat make no boost;
I make no boast of my condition;

For wel ye knowe, a lord in his houshold
For you know well, a lord in his household

Ne hath nat every vessel al of gold;   100
Does not have all his vessels of pure gold;

Somme been of tree, and doon hir lord servyse.
Some are of wood, and do their lord good service

God clepeth folk to hym in sondry wyse,
God calls folk to him in different ways,

And everich hath of God a propre yifte,
And each has from God his own gift,

Som this, som that, as hym lyketh shifte.
Some this, some that, as he pleases to ordain it.

Virginitee is greet perfeccion,   105
Virginity is a great perfection,

And continence eek with devocion,
And so is devout continence,

But Crist, that of perfeccion is welle,
But Christ, who is the source of perfection,

Bat nat every wight he sholde go selle
Did not order everyone to go and sell

Al that he hadde and yeve it to the poore
All that he had and give it to the poor

And in swich wise folwe hym and his foore.   110
And in such things follow him and his path.

Pilgrim with Wallet and Staff

89. "fyr and tow": tow, a sort of hemp, was highly inflammable. The phrase is proverbial.

101. The example comes from II Timothy 2:20.

THE WIFE OF BATH

[Lines 111-134]

Although the Wife is not aware of it, Chaucer makes her assertions about virginity, marriage, and procreation a part of a much larger debate which lay behind a great many of the medieval sermons, homilies, and theological arguments.

One of the central conflicts in the religious thought of the time lay between two views of the world: on the one hand it was an ephemeral, evil temptation, whose delights were a barrier to man's fulfillment in the next world; on the other hand, since the world was divinely created and ordered, its values were real and good.

Reduced to the relation between the sexes, the first view was obliged to condemn marriage as a worldly, sensual trap; the second endorsed marriage and reproduction as the working out of God's plan for the created world.

The Wife would not understand the theological ramifications of this debate, and her phrasing is hardly philosophical (the organs of reproduction are, she says, "to purge uryne and eek for engendrure"), but she is a representative of the second view. Chaucer's brilliance here is in making the defender of this view not a thinker at all but the very embodiment of what she defends—the life of instinct. She may be coarse and vulgar and selfish, but she is alive and cannot be denied.

He spak to hem that wolde lyve parfitly—
He spoke to them that would live perfectly—

And lordynges, by youre leve, that am nat I!
And masters, by your leave, such am not I!

I wol bistowe the flour of al myn age
I will bestow the flower of all my years

In th' actes and in fruyt of mariage.
In the acts and the fruit of marriage.

Telle me also, to what conclusion   115
Tell me also, to what end

Were membres maad of generacion,
Were the organs of generation made,

And of so parfit wys a wight ywroght?
And a person so perfectly designed?

Trusteth right wel, they were nat maad for noght.
Trust to it, they were not made for nothing.

Glose whoso wole, and seye bothe up and doun
Interpret whoever will, and say it up and down

That they were maked for purgacioun   120
That they were made for the elimination

Of uryne, and oure bothe thynges smale
Of urine, and both our little things

Were eek to knowe a femele from a male,
Were there to tell a female from a male,

And for noon oother cause—sey ye no?
And for no other cause—do you say no?

Th' experience woot wel it is noght so.
Experience tells us it is not so.

So that the clerkes be nat with me wrothe,   125
So that the scholars are not angry with me,

I sey this, that they maked been for bothe,
I say this, that they are made for both,

That is to seye, for office and for ese
That is to say, for function and for pleasure

Of engendrure, ther we nat God displese.
Of generation, where we do not displease God.

Why sholde men elles in hir bookes sette
Why else should men say in their books

That man shal yelde to his wyf hir dette?   130
That man should pay his debt to his wife?

Now wherwith sholde he make his paiement,
Now with what will he make his payment,

If he ne used his sely instrument?
Unless he use his blessed instrument?

Thanne were they maad upon a creature
So they were created on a person

To purge uryne, and eek for engendrure.
To purge urine, and for generation.

Sitting under "The Word"

130. This notion of "debt" comes from I Corinthians 7:3.

22

But I seye noght that every wight is holde, 135
But I do not say that every person is bound,

That hath switch harneys as I to yow tolde,
That possesses such parts as I tell you of,

To goon and usen hem in engendrure;
To go and use them for begetting;

Thanne sholde men take of chastitee no cure.
Then men would take no heed of chastity.

Crist was a mayde and shapen as a man,
Christ was a virgin, and made as a man,

And many a seint sith that the world bigan; 140
And many a saint, since the world began;

Yet lyved they evere in parfit chastitee.
Yet they lived always in perfect chastity.

I nyl envye no virginitee;
I do not envy any virginity;

Lat hem be breed of pured whete seed,
Let them be bread of pure wheat seed

And lat us wyves hote barly breed;
And let us wives be called barley bread;

And yet with barly breed, Mark telle kan, 145
And yet with barley bread, as Mark can tell,

Oure Lord Jhesu refresshed many a man.
Our Lord Jesus refreshed many a man.

In swich estaat as God hath cleped us
In such estate as God has called us to

I wol persevere; I nam nat precius.
I will persevere; I am not fastidious.

In wyfhode wol I use myn instrument
In wifehood I will use my instrument

As frely as my Makere hath it sent. 150
As freely as my Maker has given it.

If I be daungerous, God yeve me sorwe!
If I be grudging, God give me sorrow!

Myn housbonde shal it have bothe eve and morwe,
My husband shall have it both night and morning,

Whan that hym list come forth and paye his dette.
When he wants to come forth and pay his debt.

An housbonde wol I have, I wol nat lette,
A husband I will have, I will not desist,

Which shal be bothe my dettour and my thral, 155
Who shall be both my debtor and my slave,

And have his tribulacion withal
And have his troubles as well

Upon his flessh while that I am his wyf.
Upon his flesh while I am his wife.

I have the power duryng al my lyf
I have the authority through all my life

143. In the Middle Ages there were various sorts of bread, of different quality and price. Virgins are compared to bread made from "pured," or purified wheat. Wives are an inferior sort, bread made from barley flour. The comparison suggests that, although inferior, wives have an important, if earthly, function to fulfill.

145. The story of the loaves feeding five thousand is actually from St. John.

Tally Sticks

THE WIFE OF BATH

[Lines 159-182]

At 163 the Wife is interrupted by the Pardoner. Such interruptions occur regularly in the course of the Canterbury Tales, and although they always seem to be accidental and unpremeditated, or "realistic," they are carefully staged by Chaucer. Usually they serve two purposes, as is the case here.

First, they remind us that we are dealing with a group. The Wife has gone on for more than 160 lines, which is long enough to make us lose sight of the rest of Chaucer's pilgrims.

But the Canterbury Tales is itself the tale of a whole society and not of any one individual. The interruptions and debates make us aware again of the fact that we have here not one point of view, but many; not a single attitude, but a variety of attitudes. The Wife may think one thing, but there is always a Pardoner, or a Friar or a Summoner who thinks something else.

Second, an interruption such as we have here serves a dramatic purpose. A large part of the appeal of Chaucer's work is its dramatic juxtaposition of different and often conflicting types. They have all been presented in the General Prologue, but as the tales unfold, we watch them interact.

The process is best described by J. L. Lowes: "'Antagonisms flame up; a drunken pilgrim insists on telling his tale out of turn; the Shipman flatly refuses to hear a sermon from the Parson and promises a tale that will wake the company up; a cleric drinks too much ale and his tongue is unclerically loosed; a lively discussion of marriage springs up and tales, informative and lively, are told in support of divergent views. The company, in a word, that gathered in Southwark at the Tabard were there in precisely the position of any shipload of travellers as the ship leaves port.''

Upon his propre body, and nat he:
Upon his own body, and not he:

Right thus th' Apostle tolde it unto me;   160
Just as the Apostle told it to me;

And bad oure housbondes for to love us weel.
And told our husbands to love us well.

Al this sentence me liketh every deel."
All this judgment pleases me."

Up stirte the Pardoner and that anon:
Up jumped the Pardoner at once:

"Now dame," quod he, "by God and by Seint John,
"Now madam," he said, "by God and by Saint John,

Ye been a noble prechour in this cas!   165
You are a noble preacher in this matter!

I was aboute to wedde a wyf; allas,
I was about to wed a wife; alas,

What sholde I bye it on my flessh so deere?
Why should I pay so dearly for it with my flesh?

Yet hadde I levere wedde no wyf to yeere!"
Now would I rather wed no wife this year!"

"Abyde," quod she, "my tale is nat bigonne.
"Wait," she said, "my tale is not begun.

Nay, thow shalt drynken of another tonne,   170
No, you shall drink from another cask,

Er that I go, shal savoure wors than ale.
Before I go, that will taste worse than ale.

And whan that I have toold thee forth my tale
And when I have told you my story

Of tribulacion in mariage,
Of tribulation in marriage,

Of which I am expert in al myn age—
Of which I am the expert of my time—

This is to seye, myself hath been the whippe—   175
That is to say, I myself have been the whip—

Thanne maystow chese wheither thou wolt sippe
Then you may choose whether you care to sip

Of thilke tonne that I shal abroche.
Of the cask that I shall tap.

Be war of it, er thou too neigh approche;
Be careful of it, before you come too close;

For I shal telle ensamples mo than ten.
For I shall tell examples more than ten.

'Whoso that nyl be war by othere men,   180
'Whose will not be warned by other men,

By hym shal othere men corrected be.'
By him shall other men be warned.'

Thise same wordes writeth Ptholomee;
These are the words that Ptolemy writes;

The Pardoner

160. St. Paul is the Wife's authority for both these statements.

180-84. The Wife, or Chaucer, is mistaken here, since this aphorism does not occur in Ptolemy's Almagest, but elsewhere in his writings. Ptolemy was an astronomer of the second century and his most famous work, the Almagest, was well known to the Middle Ages.

THE WIFE OF BATH

[Lines 183-206]

We have already met the Pardoner in the General Prologue. He is one of the most scurrilous members of the party, a cleric authorized to sell papal indulgences to sinners, which was a right widely abused in the Middle Ages. His wallet, Chaucer tells us, is "bretful of pardon, comen from Rome al hoot," and he is able to convince the peasantry that an old pillowcase is the Virgin's veil and a bag of "pigges bones" are the remains, or relics, of the saints. We are liable to distrust anything he says, and Chaucer does not disappoint us.

In the General Prologue the Pardoner is presented as effeminate, to such a degree that Chaucer says "I trowe he were a geldyng or a mare." Therefore there is an elaborate and entirely conscious irony in his statement that he is "'aboute to wedde a wyf, allas," which is redoubled a few lines later when he pretends to need instruction in the art of marriage: "teche us yonge men of youre praktike."

Rede in his Almageste and take it there."
Read in his Almagest and see it there."

"Dame, I wolde praye yow, if youre wyl it were,"
"Madam, I beg you, if you are willing,"

Seyde this Pardoner, "as ye bigan,   185
Said this Pardoner, "as you have begun,

Telle forth youre tale; spareth for no man,
Tell forth your tale; spare no man,

And teche us yonge men of youre praktike."
And teach us young men from your experience."

"Gladly," quod she, "sith it may you like;
"Gladly," said she, "since you may enjoy it;

But that I praye to al this compaignye,
But yet I ask all this company,

If that I speke after my fantasye,   190
If I speak after my fancy,

As taketh nat agrief of that I seye,
Do not take what I say amiss,

For myn entente nys but for to pleye.
For my intent is only to give pleasure.

Now sire, thanne wol I telle yow forth my tale.
Now sirs, now I will tell my story.

As evere moote I drynke wyn or ale,
As ever I hope to drink wine or ale,

I shal seye sooth: tho housbondes that I hadde,   195
I shall speak truth: those husbands that I had,

As three of hem were goode, and two were badde.
Three of them were good, and two were bad.

The thre were goode men, and riche, and olde;
The three men were good, and rich, and old;

Unnethe myghte they the statut holde
They could hardly hold the statute

In which that they were bounden unto me—
By which they were bound to me—

Ye woot wel what I mene of this, pardee!   200
You know well what I mean by this, indeed!

As help me God, I laughe whan I thynke
So help me God I laugh when I remember

How pitously anyght I made hem swynke!
How pitifully at night I made them work!

And by my fey, I tolde of it no stoor.
And by my faith, I set not store by it.

They hadde me yeven hir land and hir tresoor;
They had given me their land and their wealth;

Me neded nat do lenger diligence   205
I had no need for further diligence

To wynne hir love or doon hem reverence.
To win their love or pay them respect.

198. "the statut holde": hold, or obey the statute, with reference to line 130.

Domineering Wife

They loved me so wel, by God above,
They loved me so well, by God above,

That I ne tolde no deyntee of hir love.
That I set no value on their love.

A wys womman wol bisye hire evere in oon
A wise woman will busy herself constantly

To gete hir love, ye, ther as she hath noon.   210
To win love, when she has none.

But sith I hadde hem hoolly in myn hond,
But since I had them completely in hand,

And sith they hadde yeven me al hir lond,
And since they had given me all their land,

What sholde I take kepe hem for to plese,
Why should I take pains to please them,

But it were for my profit and myn ese?
Except for my own profit and pleasure?

I sette hem so awerke, by my fey,   215
I put them so to work, by my faith,

That many a nyght they songen 'weilaway!'
That many a night they cried 'woe is me!'

The bacon was nat fet for hem, I trowe,
The bacon was not fetched for them, I believe,

That som men han in Essexe at Dunmowe.
That some men have in Essex and Dunmow.

I governed hem so wel after my lawe,
I governed them so well, according to my law,

That ech of hem ful blisful was and fawe   220
That each of them was very happy and eager

To brynge me gaye thynges fro the fayre;
To bring me gay things from the fair;

They were ful glad whan I spak to hem faire,
They were most pleased when I spoke fairly to them,

For God it woot, I chidde hem spitously.
For God knows I nagged them harshly.

  Now herkneth how I bar me proprely,
  Now listen how I behaved myself properly,

Ye wise wyves, that kan understonde,   225
You wise wives, that can understand,

Thus sholde ye speke and bere hem wrong on honde;
Thus should you speak and put them in the wrong;

For half so boldely kan ther no man
For half so boldly can no man

Swere and lyen as a woman kan.
Swear and lie as a woman can.

I sey nat this by wyves that been wyse,
I do not say this for wives who are wise,

But if it be whan they hem mysavyse.   230
Unless it be when they act ill-advisedly.

217-18. During the reign of Henry II it was ordered that any married couple who had not quarreled within a year of their marriage might go to the Priory at Dunmow, in Essex, and claim a flitch of bacon.

One of the longest sections of the prologue has to do with the way in which the Wife dealt with her first three husbands. Of all the five, she says, "three of hem were goode, and two were badde." This is a judgment the reader qualifies somewhat later on, for it appears that the "bad" mates, the nameless "revelour" and Jenkin, she really did love.

The first three were good in a somewhat limited sense: they were all "riche, and olde." The Wife's treatment of them was merciless, and she takes a good deal of pleasure in recalling it. She was young and attractive, and they were old, and control over them was a simple matter: "I hadde hem hoolly in myn hond."

THE WIFE OF BATH

[Lines 231-254]

This control was partly a matter of her physical attraction and partly barefaced bullying. She "chidde hem spitously" on every possible topic. She has not as many, or as grand, clothes as her neighbor. She is not allowed to have a "gossip," or friend. She is falsely suspected of flirting with the husband's apprentice. She is not allowed to have any money. The Wife is indeed, as she says, the "whippe" that punishes the spouses.

Yet in the midst of this Chaucer cleverly interweaves the husbands'—or the male—response by having the Wife quote them, for example at 257-64, and elsewhere. This sets up something like a dialogue and throughout this section, as in the section dealing with Jenkin's book (669-787), we get an alternation between a wife's vilification of her husband and his denunciation of her.

Here again we are dealing, not with a single situation, but with a lengthy and pervasive medieval debate. The anti-feminism of Jerome's *Epistle* is only one example of a large anti-feminist literature. Nor was this confined to scholarly and intellectual argument.

The sermons of the period, delivered to the general populace, were full of reminders that Adam fell through Eve's sin and that women, alternately with money, were the root of all evil.

Contemporary woodcuts illustrating popular fables often showed a man and a woman tugging at a pair of breeches which symbolized dominance—the early forerunner of our own phrase about who "wears the pants in the family."

Chaucer, as might be expected, embodied several points of view in his *Canterbury Tales*; the domineering Wife is balanced, for example, by Patient Griselda of the Clerk's tale.

However, the Wife's uncompromising attitude may in part be accounted for by a tale told earlier in the series. The Nun's Priest had seemed to be a gentle and diffident person, the last who might be expected to give offense. His

A wys wyf shal, if that she kan hir good,
A wise wife shall, if she knows her own good,

Bere hym on honde that the cow is wood,
Make him believe that the crow is mad,

And take witnesse of hir owene mayde
And use as witness her own maid

Of hir assent. But herkneth how I sayde:
For her statement. But hear what I used to say:

'Sire olde kaynard, is this thyn array?   235
'Sir old fogy, is this your way?

Why is my neighebores wyf so gay?
Why is my neighbor's wife so gaily dressed?

She is honoured over al ther she gooth;
She is honored everywhere she goes;

I sitte at hoom; I have no thrifty cloth.
I sit at home; I have no good clothes.

What dostow at my neighebores hous?
What do you do at my neighbor's house?

Is she so fair? Artow so amorous?   240
Is she so fair? Are you so amorous?

What rowne ye with oure mayde, *benedicite?*
What are you whispering with our maid? Bless us!

Sire olde lechour, lat thy japes be!
Old sir lecher, stop your tricks!

And if I have a gossib or a freend,
And if I have a confidant or a friend,

Withouten gilt thou chidest as a feend,
Though I am guiltless, you chide like a devil,

If that I walke or pleye unto his hous.   245
If I go to his house for amusement.

Thou comest hoom as dronken as a mous,
You come home as drunk as a mouse,

And prechest on thy bench, with yvel preef!
And preach from your bench, bad luck to you!

Thou seist to me, it is a greet mescheef
You tell me it is a great mistake

To wedde a povre womman for costage;
To wed a poor woman because of the cost;

And if that she be riche, of heigh parage,   250
And if she be rich, of noble birth,

Thanne seistow that it is a tormentrye
Then you say it is a torment

To suffre hir pride and hir malencolye.
To suffer her pride and her bad moods.

And if that she be fair, thou verray knave,
And if she be fair, you true peasant,

Thou seist that every holour wol hire have;
You say that every lecher wants her;

232. "the cow is wood": the "cow" is the chough, or crow, and the illusion is to the old story of the bird who tells the jealous husband that his wife is unfaithful. The wife persuades him that the bird is lying. Chaucer has a version of the story in the Manciple's tale.

241. "benedicite": the blessing is pronounced in three syllables, ben-si-te.

246. "dronken as a mous": this was a proverbial expression, later replaced by "drunk as a rat," and later still by "drunk as a goat."

The Canterbury Ampulla

THE WIFE OF BATH

[Lines 255-278]

tale, however, turned out to contain a good deal of sharp anti-feminism and retailed many of the popular arguments against women, including the one that makes them responsible for the fall of man:

"Wommenes conseils been ful ofte colde;
And made Adam fro Paradys to go,
There as he was ful meryie and wel at ese."

The Canterbury Tales contain some dramatic clashes, and this may be an implicit one. One can imagine the Wife directing some of her more sulfurous denunciations of men at the Nun's Priest, and particularly that passage where she comments on those members of the clergy who write about marriage:

"The clerk, whan he is old and may noght do
Of Venus werkes worth his olde sho,
Thanne sit he doun and writ in his dotage
That wommen kan nat kepe hir mariage!"

FEMINIST QUALITIES

She may no while in chastitee abyde   255
That she cannot long be chaste

That is assailled upon ech a syde.
Who is assailed on every side.

Thou seyst som folk desire us for richesse,
You say some men desire us for wealth,

Some for oure shape, and somme for oure fairnesse,
Some for our figure, and some for our beauty,

And som for she kan outher synge or daunce,
And some for talent in either song or dance,

And som for gentilesse and daliaunce,   260
And some for breeding and flirtation,

Som for hir handes and hir armes smale:
Some for slender hands and arms:

Thus goth al to the devel by thy tale!
Thus all go to the devil according to you!

Thou seyst men may nat kepe a castel wal,
You say men cannot protect a castle wall,

It may so longe assailled been over al.
So constantly attacked from every side.

And if that she be foul, thou seist that she   265
And if she be ugly, you say that she

Coveiteth every man that she may se,
Covets every man she sees,

For as a spanyel she wol on hym lepe,
For like a spaniel she will on him leap,

Til that she fynde som man hire to chepe.
Until she find some man to take her.

Ne noon so grey goos gooth ther in the lake,
Nor is there any goose swims in the lake,

As, seistow, wol be withoute make;   270
That, you say, will be without a mate;

And seyst it is an hard thyng for to welde
And you say it is a hard thing to control

A thyng that no man wol, his thankes, helde.
A thing that no man wants willingly to hold.

Thus seistow, lorel, whan thow goost to bedde;
So you speak, wretch, when you go to bed;

And that no wys man nedeth for to wedde,
And that no wise man need wed,

Ne no man that entendeth unto hevene—   275
Nor any man who aims to go to heaven—

With wilde thonder-dynt and firy levene
With the wild thunder-bolt and fiery lightning

Moote thy welked nekke be tobroke!
May your wrinkled neck be broken!

Thou seyst that droppyng houses and eek smoke
You say that leaking houses and also smoke

272. "a thyng": i.e., a woman.

28

And chidyng wyves maken men to flee
And nagging wives make men flee

Out of hir owene houses. A, *benedicite!*   280
From their own houses. Ah, bless us!

What eyleth swich an old man for to chide?
What ails such an old man to scold so?

 Thow seyst we wyves wil oure vices hide
 You say we women hide our vices

Til we be fast, and thanne we wol hem shewe—
Until we are secure, and then we show them—

Wel may that be a proverbe of a shrewe!
Certainly that is the proverb of a scoundrel!

 Thou seist that oxen, asses, hors, and houndes,   285
 You say that oxen, asses, horses and hounds,

They been assayed at diverse stoundes,
Are tested at various times,

Bacyns, lavours, er that men hem bye,
Basins, washbowls, before men buy them,

Spoones and stooles, and al swich housbondrye,
Spoons and stools, and all such furnishings,

And so be pottes, clothes, and array;
And so are pots, cloth and garments;

But folk of wyves maken noon assay   290
But men make no test of wives

Til they be wedded—olde dotard shrewe!
Until they are married—evil old dotard!

And thanne, seistow, we wil oure vices shewe.
And then, you say, we show our vices.

 Thou seist also that it displeseth me
 You say also that I am displeased

But if that thou wolt preise my beautee,
Unless you praise my beauty,

And but thou poure alwey upon my face,   295
And unless you continually gaze at my face,

And clepe me "Faire Dame" in every place;
And call me "Fair Lady" in every place;

And but thou make a feeste on thilke day
And unless you arrange a feast on that day

That I was born, and make me fressh and gay;
That I was born, and dress me fresh and gay;

And but thou do to my norice honour,
And unless you honor my nurse,

And to my chamberere withinne my bour,   300
And the maid of my chamber,

And to my fadres folk, and his allyes—
And to my father's people and his friends—

Thus seistow, olde barel-ful of lyes!
Thus you speak, old barrel-full of lies!

283. "fast": i.e., married, and therefore not afraid of consequences.

Slip-Ware Jug

THE WIFE OF BATH

[Lines 303-326]

And yet of oure apprentice Janekyn,
And yet of our apprentice Jenkin,

For his crispe heer, shynyng as gold so fyn,
Because of his crisp hair, shining as fine as gold,

And for he squiereth me bothe up and doun,   305
And because he escorts me up and down,

Yet hastow caught a fals suspecioun.
You have caught a false suspicion.

I wil hym nat thogh thou were deed tomorwe!
I do not want him though you died tomorrow!

But tel me this, why hydestow, with sorwe,
But tell me this, why do you hide, bad luck to you,

The keyes of thy cheste away fro me?
The keys of your money box from me?

It is my good as wel as thyn, pardee!   310
It is my wealth as well as yours, by heaven!

What, wenestow make an ydiot of oure dame?
What, do you think to make a fool of your wife?

Now by that lord that called is Seint Jame,
Now by that lord called Saint James,

Thou shalt nat bothe, thogh that thow were wood,
You shall not, even though you rage,

Be maister of my body and of my good;
Be master of my body and my property;

That oon thou shalt forgo, maugree thyne eyen.   315
One you shall do without, curse your eyes.

What helpeth it of me to enquere and spyen?
Why do you need to question and spy on me?

I trowe thou woldest loke me in thy chiste!
I swear you would lock me in your box!

Thou sholdest seye, "Wyf, go wher thee liste;
You should say, "Wife go where you like;

Taak youre disport, I wol nat leve no talys.
Take your pleasure, I will believe no tales.

I knowe yow for a trewe wyfe, dame Alys."   320
I know you are a faithful wife, lady Alice."

We love no man that taketh kepe or charge
We love no man that notices and oversees

Wher that we goon; we wol been at oure large.
Where we go; we want to be free.

Of alle men yblessed moot he be,
Of all men blessed may he be,

The wise astrologen daun Ptholomee,
The wise astrologer lord Ptolemy,

That seith this proverbe in his Almageste: 325
Who speaks this proverb in his Almagest:

"Of alle men his wisdom is hyeste
"Of all men his wisdom is the highest,

Widow's Barb

That rekketh nat who hath the world in honde."
Who does not care who has the world in hand."

By this proverbe thow shalt understonde,
By this proverb you are to understand,

Have thow ynogh, what thar thee rekke or care
If you have enough, what need to worry

How myrily that othere folkes fare?   330
How merrily other folk fare?

For certes, olde dotard, by youre leve,
For certainly, old dotard, by your leave,

Ye shal have queynte right ynogh at eve.
You will have enough of it at night.

He is too greet a nygard that wil werne
He is too selfish that will forbid

A man to lighte a candle at his lanterne;
A man to light a candle at his lantern;

He shal have never the lasse lighte, pardee.   335
He shall not have the less light, by heaven.

Have thou ynogh, thee thar nat pleyne thee.
If you have enough, no need for you to complain.

Thou seist also that if we make us gay
You also say that if we make ourselves gay

With clothyng and with precious array,
With clothes and expensive outfitting,

That it is peril of oure chastitee;
That it endangers our chastity;

And yet, with sorwe, thou most enforce thee,   340
*And yet, bad luck to you, you must reinforce your
claim,*

And seye thise wordes in th' Apostles name:
And say these words in the Apostle's name:

"In habit maad with chastitee and shame
"In clothing made chastely and modestly,

Ye wommen shal apparaille yow," quod he,
You women shall dress yourselves," said he,

"And nat in tressed heer and gay perree,
*"And not in elaborately dressed hair and gay
jewelry,*

As perles, ne with gold, ne clothes riche."   345
Such as pearls, nor with gold, nor with rich clothes";

After thy text, ne after thy rubriche,
For your text, and your direction,

I wol nat werke as muchel as a gnat.
I will live by it as much as a gnat would.

Thou seydest this, that I was lyk a cat;
You said this, that I was like a cat;

For whoso wolde senge a cattes skyn,
For whoever would singe a cat's fur,

341. From I Timothy 2:9.

Bronze Brooch

The Eyes of Argus Were Cast
into a Peacock's Tail

Thanne wolde the cat wel dwellen in his in;　　350
Would have the cat live happily in his home;

And if the cattes skyn be slyk and gay,
And if the cat's fur is sleek and handsome,

She wol nat dwelle in house half a day,
She will not stay in the house half a day,

But forth she wole, er any day be dawed,
But will go out, before daybreak,

To shewe her skyn and goon a-caterwawed.
To show off her fur and caterwaul.

This is to seye, if I be gay, sire shrewe,　　355
This is to say, if I am gayly dressed, sir scoundrel,

I wol renne out, my borel for to shewe.
I will run out to show off my clothing.

　Sire olde fool, what helpeth thee t'espyen?
　Sir old fool, what does it help you to spy?

Thogh thow preye Argus with his hundred eyen
Though you beg Argus with his hundred eyes,

To be my warde-cors, as he kan best,
To be my bodyguard, as he best knows how,

In feith, he shal nat kepe me but me lest;　　360
In faith, he will not hold me unless I allow it;

Yet koude I make his berd, so mote I thee.
As I could outwit him, so I can you.

　Thou seydest eek that ther been thynges three,
　You also said that there are three things,

The whiche thynges troublen al this erthe,
Which trouble all this earth,

And that no wight may endure the ferthe.
And that no man can endure the fourth.

O leeve sire shrewe, Jhesu shorte thy lyf!　　365
O dear sir scoundrel, Jesus shorten thy life!

Yet prechestow and seist an hateful wyf
Yet you preach and say that a hateful wife

Yrekened is for oon of thise myschaunces.
Is reckoned as one of these misfortunes.

Been ther none othere maner resemblaunces
Are there no other sort of similarities

That ye may likne youre parables to,
That you can apply your parables to,

But if a sely wyf be one of tho?　　370
Unless an innocent wife be one of them?

　Thou liknest eek wommanes love to helle,
　You compare woman's love to hell,

To bareyne land ther water may nat dwelle;
To barren land where water cannot stay;

Thow liknest it also to wilde fyr;
You compare it also to wildfire;

358. Argus was a monster with a hundred eyes, and since some of these were always open, regarded as the ideal guardian.

362. From Proverbs 30:21-23: "For three things the earth is disquieted, and four which it cannot bear: For a servant when he reigneth; and a fool when he is filled with meat; for an odious woman when she is married; and an handmaid that is heir to her mistress."

[Lines 374-397]

The moore it brenneth, the moore it hath desir
The more it burns, the more it wants

To consume every thyng that brent wol be. 375
To consume everything that can be burned.

Thow seist right as wormes shende a tree,
You say that just as worms destroy a tree,

Right so a wyf destroyeth hir housbonde;
So a wife destroys her husband;

This knowen they that been to wyves bonde.'
This they know who have been bound to wives.'

Lordinges, right thus, as ye have understonde,
Masters, just so, as you have learned,

Bar I stifly myne olde housbondes on honde 380
I boldly accused my old husbands

That thus they seyden in hir dronkenesse;
That they said these things in their drunkenness;

And al was fals, but that I took witnesse
And it was all false, but I called as witnesses

On Janekyn and on my nece also.
Jenkin and my niece as well.

O Lord, the peyne I dide hem and the wo,
O Lord, the pain I caused them and the woe,

Ful giltelees, by Goddes sweete pyne! 385
Quite guiltless, by God's sweet suffering!

For as an hors I koude byte and whyne;
For I could bite and whinny like a horse;

I koude pleyne thogh I were in the gilt,
I could complain even though I was wrong,

Or elles often tyme I hadde been split.
Or else often I would have been ruined.

Whoso that first to mille comth, first grynt;
Who comes to the mill first, grinds first;

I pleyned first, so was oure werre stynt. 390
I complained first, so our warfare was ended.

They were ful glad to excusen hem ful blyve
They were glad enough to excuse themselves quickly

Of thyng of which they nevere agilte hir lyve.
Of that which they were never guilty of in their lives.

Of wenches wolde I beren hem on honde,
I would accuse my husband of women

Whan that for syk they myghte unnethe stonde;
When he could hardly stand for sickness;

Yet tikled it his herte for that he 395
Yet it pleased his heart, because he

Wende that I hadde of hym so greet chiertee.
Believed that I held so much fondness for him.

I swoor that al my walkyng out by nyghte
I swore that all my walking out at night

Street Shop

385. "sweete pyne": Christ's suffering on the Cross is called "sweet" because it redeemed man's sin and provided for his salvation.

Readers have sometimes been offended by the outright phrasing of the Wife's marital reminiscences, here and elsewhere. Many editions omit those lines containing suggestive references, just as they omit whole tales—such as the Miller's and the Reeve's—which deal with the bald facts of man's physical existence.

This points to one of the great differences between the twentieth and the fourteenth centuries. We find it hard to believe that such characters as the Miller and the Wife of Bath, who speak with such brutal directness about matters we consider unmentionable, would go on a pilgrimage to the shrine of St. Thomas of Canterbury. But they did go, and Chaucer nowhere suggests that their belief was hypocritical.

In many ways the medieval attitude was wider and more flexible than ours, and this accounts for the fact that they were not shocked by the sort of reference the Wife and the Miller make. The Wife's sexual references, like those in the Bible, are totally free of any pornographic overtones.

She is speaking of matters of fact in a matter-of-fact way, and there is no question of editing or suppressing for the benefit of such listeners as the Prioress or the Second Nun. The medieval mind credited them with being able to accept such matters of fact.

Was for to espye wenches that he dighte;
Was to spy on women that he lay with;

Under that colour hadde I many a myrthe.
Under color of that I had many a laugh.

For al swich wit is yeven us in oure birthe;   400
For all such wit is given us at our birth;

Deceite, wepyng, spynnyng God hath yive
Deceit, weeping, spinning, God has given

To wommen kyndely whil they may lyve.
To women by their nature as long as they live.

And thus of o thyng I avaunte me:
And so of one thing I boast:

Atte ende I hadde the bet in ech degree,
In the end I had it better in every way,

By sleighte or force, or by som maner thyng,   405
By trick, or force, or by some kind of device,

As by continuel murmur of grucchyng.
As by continually nagging and grumbling.

Namely abedde hadden they meschaunce:
Especially in bed they had a bad time:

Ther wolde I chide and do hem no plesaunce;
There I would nag and give them no pleasure;

I wolde no lenger in the bed abyde
I would no longer remain in bed

If that I felte his arm over my syde,   410
If I felt his arm over my side,

Til he had maad his raunson unto me;
Until he had paid his ransom to me;

Thanne wolde I suffre hym do his nycetee.
Then would I allow him to do his foolishness.

And therfore every man this tale I telle:
And therefore I tell every man this tale:

Wynne whoso may, for al is for to selle;
Let him get it who can, for everything is for sale;

With empty hand men may none haukes lure.   415
With empty hand men cannot lure hawks.

For wynnyng wolde I al his lust endure,
For profit I would endure all his lust,

And make me a feyned appetit—
And feign an appetite—

And yet in bacon hadde I nevere delit.
Yet in dried meat I never had delight.

That made me that evere I wolde hem chide;
That is what made me always nag them;

For thogh the Pope hadde seten hem biside,   420
For though the Pope had sat beside them,

I wolde nat spare hem at hir owene bord,
I would not spare them at their own table,

The Gloucester Candlestick

For by my trouthe, I quitte hem word for word.
For by my honor, I answered them word for word.

As help me verray God omnipotent,
So help me the true God omnipotent,

Though I right now sholde make my testament,
Though I should make my will right now,

I ne owe hem nat a word that it nys quit.   425
I owe them not a word that is not paid.

I broghte it so aboute by my wit
I brought it about by my wit

That they moste yeve it up as for the beste,
That they had to surrender, for the best,

Or elles hadde we nevere been in reste;
Or else we would never have had rest;

For thogh he looked as a wood leon,
For though he looked wild as a lion,

Yet sholde he faille of his conclusion.   430
Yet he would fail in his purpose.

    Thanne wolde I seye, 'Goode lief, taak keep,
    Then would I say, 'My dear, take notice,

How mekely looketh Wilkyn, oure sheep!
How meek our sheep Wilken looks!

Com neer, my spouse, lat me ba thy cheke.
Come near, my spouse, let me kiss your cheek.

Ye sholde be al pacient and meke,
You should be all patient and meek,

And han a sweete-spiced conscience,   435
And have a sweetly spiced conscience,

Sith ye so preche of Jobes pacience;
Since you preach so of Job's patience;

Suffreth alway, syn ye so wel kan preche;
Continue to suffer, since you can preach so well;

And but ye do, certeyn, we shal yow teche
Unless you do it is certain we shall teach you

That it is fair to have a wyf in pees.
How fair it is to have a wife at peace.

Oon of us two moste bowen, doutelees,   440
One of us two must give way, doubtless,

And sith a man is moore resonable
And since a man is more reasonable

Than womman is, yet mosten been suffrable.
Than woman is, you must be patient.

What eyleth yow to grucche thus and grone?
What ails you to grouch so and groan?

Is it for ye wolde have my queynte allone?
*Is it because you would have my pudendum all to
     yourself?*

432. "Wilkyn": presumably the name of a pet sheep; not a very flattering comparison on the Wife's part.

[Lines 445-468]

The Wife's situation changes somewhat with her last two husbands. The fourth husband has a "paramour" and is not entirely hers, thus illustrating the Wife's ancient psychological dictum that if something is forbidden a woman "Ther-after wol we crye al-day and crave."

It is one of the disarming things about the Wife of Bath that, although she defends herself with vigor, she never apologizes for or excuses her misdemeanors. One can imagine what an author of a later date might have made out of the noble suffering of the injured wife in this situation.

Chaucer is too wise to falsify her character; by now we know her, and we know just what she would do faced with a "paramour," and she does it. She punishes him with suspicions of her own betrayal: "By God, in erthe I was his purgatorie."

Yet there is a sense in which she loves him, suggested by the repeated hope for his salvation, that "his soule be in glorie." There is perhaps no more revealing touch in Chaucer's presentation of the Wife than the combination of hardheaded materialism and genuine affection in the two lines that finish off the fourth husband, in which she suggests that while an expensive funeral would be wasted on him, she hopes he gains peace in heaven:

"It nys but wast to burye hym
    preciously,
Lat hym fare wel, God yeve his
    soule reste."

Wy, taak it al! Lo, have it every deel! 445
Why, take it all! Have every bit of it!

Peter, I shrewe yow but ye love it weel!
Peter, curse you but you love it well!

For if I wolde selle my *bele chose,*
For if I wanted to sell my belle chose,

I koude walke as fressh as is a rose;
I could go walking fresh as a rose;

But I wol kepe it for youre owene tooth.
But I will keep it for your own appetite.

Ye be to blame! By God, I sey yow sooth!' 450
You are to blame, by God, I tell you the truth!'

Swiche manere wordes hadde we on honde.
Words of this sort we had between us.

Now wol I speken of my fourthe housbonde.
Now I will talk about my fourth husband.

My fourthe housbonde was a revelour;
My fourth husband was reveler;

This is to seyn, he hadde a paramour;
That is to say, he had a mistress;

And I was yong and ful of ragerye, 455
And I was young and full of passion,

Stibourne and strong and joly as a pie.
Stubborn and strong, and merry as a magpie.

How koude I daunce to an harpe smale,
How I could dance to a small harp,

And synge, ywis, as any nyghtyngale,
And sing, I tell you, like any nightingale,

Whan I had dronke a draughte of sweete wyn!
When I had drunk a draught of sweet wine!

Metellius, the foule cherl, the swyn, 460
Metellius, the foul peasant, the swine,

That with a staf birafte his wyf hir lyf
That with his staff beat his wife to death

For she drank wyn, though I hadde been his wyf,
Because she drank wine, if I had been his wife,

He sholde nat han daunted me fro drynke!
He should not have frightened me from drink!

And after wyn on Venus moste I thynke,
And after wine on Venus most I think,

For al so siker as cold engendreth hayl, 465
For just as sure as cold produces hail,

A likerous mouth moste han a likerous tayl;
A greedy mouth must have a licentious tail;

In womman vinolent is no defence
Wine drinking in women is no hindrance—

This knowen lechours by experience.
Lechers know this by experience.

Covered Cup

THE WIFE OF BATH

[Lines 469-492]

It is significant that the Wife's courtship of Jenkin, the "som tyme clerk of Oxenford," goes on while her fourth husband is still alive. At the funeral she pretends to weep, but her eyes are on Jenkin and "al myn herte I yaf unto his hoold." In a lesser writer such a passage would inevitably turn into an attack on the Wife's lack of feeling, but what Chaucer stresses is the presence, not the absence of feeling; she is passionately committed to life and therefore to the living.

But Lord Crist! whan that it remembreth me
But Lord Christ! when my mind goes back

Upon my youthe and on my jolitee,   470
To my youth and my gaiety,

It tikleth me aboute myn herte roote;
It tickles me to the bottom of my heart;

Unto this day it dooth myn herte boote
To this day it does my heart good

That I have had my world as in my tyme.
That I have had my world in my own time.

But age, allas, that al wole envenyme,
But age, alas, that will envenom everything,

Hath me biraft my beautee and my pith.   475
Has taken from me my beauty and my vigor.

Lat go, farewel, the devel go therwith!
Let it go, farewell, the devil go with it!

The flour is goon, ther is namoore to telle;
The flour is gone, there is no more to say;

The bren, as I best kan, now moste I selle;
Now must I sell the bran as best I can;

But yet to be right murye wol I fonde.
Yet to be right merry I will try.

Now wol I tellen of my fourthe housbonde.   480
Now will I tell of my fourth husband.

I saye I hadde in herte greet despit
As I said, I had great resentment in my heart

That he of any oother had delit.
That he had delight in any other.

But he was quit, by God and by Seint Joce!
But he was paid back, by God and by Saint Joce!

I made hym of the same wode a croce—
I made him a cross of the same wood—

Nat of my body in no foul manere—   485
Not of my body in any foul way—

But, certeinly, I made folk swich cheere
But truly, I appeared so gay to people

That in his owene grece I made hym frye
That I made him fry in his own grease

For angre and for verray jalousye.
With anger and with real jealousy.

By God, in erthe I was his purgatorie,
By God, I was his purgatory on earth,

For which I hope his soule be in glorie.   490
For which I hope his soul may be in glory.

For, God it woot, he sat ful ofte and song
For, God knows, he sat often enough and sang

Whan that his shoo ful bitterly hym wrong.
When his shoe pinched him bitterly.

469-73. These lines are often quoted as the best expression of the Wife's view of life, and perhaps Chaucer's. However, they closely follow a speech of La Vieille in Le Roman de la Rose. See Commentary.

Essay on Wifes unapologetic accounts of her past afraid of being old

483. "Seint Joce": a Breton saint, Judocus, but here probably chosen for the rhyme.

484. "of the same wode": i.e., I made him suffer in the way he had made me suffer.

Coins of Chaucer's Time

Ther was no wight, save God and he, that wiste
There was no one, except he and God, who knew

In many wise how soore I hym twiste.
In how many ways and how sharply I tortured him.

He deyde whan I cam fro Jerusalem,   495
He died when I came back from Jerusalem,

And lith ygrave under the roode-beem,
And lies buried under the rood-beem,

Al is his tombe noght so curyous
Although his tomb is not so elaborate

As was the sepulcre of hym Daryus,
As was the sepulcher of Darius,

Which that Appelles wroghte subtilly;
That which Apelles carved intricately;

It nys but wast to burye hym preciously.   500
It was nothing but waste to bury him expensively.

Lat hym fare wel, God yeve his soule reste;
May he fare well, God give rest to his soul;

He is now in his grave and in his cheste.
He is now in his grave and in his coffin.

  Now of my fifthe housbonde wol I telle.
Now I will tell of my fifth husband.

God lete his soule nevere come in helle!
God save his soul from ever going to hell!

And yet he was to me the mooste shrewe;   505
And yet he was the worst scoundrel to me;

That feele I on my ribbes al by rewe,
I can still feel the pain on my ribs,

And evere shal unto myn endyng day.
And always will, until my dying day.

But in oure bed he was so fressh and gay,
But in our bed he was so fresh and gay,

And therwithal so wel koude he me glose
And besides could flatter me so well

Whan that he wolde han my *bele chose*,   510
When he would have my belle chose,

That thogh he hadde me bet on every bon,
Though he had beaten me on every bone,

He koude wynne agayn my love anon.
He could quickly win my love again.

I trowe I loved hym best for that he
I believe I loved him best because he

Was of his love daungerous to me.
Was sparing of his love to me.

We wommen han, if that I shal nat lye,   515
We women have, if I do not lie,

In this matere a queynte fantasye:
A strange notion in this matter:

Candlestick

495. "fro Jerusalem": i.e., from her pilgrimage. "Jerusalem" is pronounced as a trisyllable, Je-ru-slem.

496. "roode-beem": a beam in the church roof running between the nave and chancel. On it there was usually a cross, or "rood." To be buried under it would be to be buried under the middle of the church floor, i.e., inexpensively.

498-99. The sepulcher of Darius was said to have been made by a Jewish artist named Apelles.

514. "daungerous": this word is complex and somewhat ambiguous in its medieval usage. It comes from the Latin *dominarius*, and may mean "domination" or "power," or in another sense, "sparing" or "unwilling to grant," as it does here.

THE WIFE OF BATH

[Lines 517-540]

The marriage with Jenkin is a bittersweet mixture of love and hostility. "I trowe I loved hym best," the Wife says, and adds that he was "fressh and gay." Yet the disagreements seem to have been violent. The Wife, by her own typically forthright admission, was stubborn "as is a leonesse" and also, as her hearers have cause to know, "of my tonge a verray jangleresse."

Jenkin, on his part, was less than chivalrous, beating her so that she will feel his blows upon her ribs "unto myn endyng day." We must recall, as the fourteenth-century reader would, that Jenkin had forfeited much in this marriage. As a cleric at Oxford he was in holy orders, and while the church relaxed its ideal of clerical celibacy somewhat for the lower orders, marriage for the higher orders was forbidden.

We are not told, of course, whether or not Jenkin was interested in furthering his clerical career, but had he been, his marriage would have blasted any hopes of doing so. This may also account for the long passage (669-787) in which Jenkin reads from his book, much to the discomfiture of the Wife.

The book, a collection of the Bible, Ovid, St. Jerome, and others, is his last connection with the world of learning and scholarship. It is an apt irony that it happens to be a collection of examples of the way in which wives bring nothing but frustration and trouble to their husbands.

Wayte what thyng we may nat lightly have,
Observe whatever thing we cannot have

The-after wol we crye al-day and crave.
We will cry all day and crave for it.

Forbede us thyng, and that desiren we;
Forbid us something, and we desire it;

Preesse on us faste, and thanne wol we fle.　　520
Urge it on us, and then we will flee.

With daunger oute we al oure chaffare;
Sparingly we set forth our merchandise;

Greet prees at market maketh deere ware,
A great crowd at market makes expensive goods,

And too greet chepe is holde at litel prys;
And too small a price is held at little value;

This knoweth every womman that is wys.
Every woman knows this who is wise.

My fifthe housbonde—God his soule blesse!—　　525
My fifth husband—God bless his soul—

Which that I took for love, and no richesse,
Whom I took for love, and not for wealth,

He som tyme was a clerk of Oxenford,
Had been once a scholar at Oxford,

And hadde left scole and wente at hom to bord
And had left school and went home to board

With my gossib, dwellyng in oure toun—
With my friend, living in our town—

God have hir soule!—hir name was Alisoun.　　530
God have her soul!—her name was Alison.

She knew myne herte and eek my privetee
She knew my heart and my secrets

Bet than oure parisshe preest, so mote I thee!
Better than our parish priest, so help me!

To hire biwreyed I my conseil al;
To her I disclosed all my confidences;

For hadde myn housbonde pissed on a wal,
For if my husband pissed on a wall,

Or doon a thyng that sholde have cost his lyf,　　535
Or did something that should have cost his life,

To hire, and to another worthy wyf,
To her, and to another worthy woman,

And to my nece which that I loved weel,
And to my niece, whom I loved well,

I wolde han toold his conseil every deel.
I would have told every bit of his secret.

And so I dide ful often, God it woot,
And so I very often did, God knows,

That made his face often reed and hoot　　540
Which made his face very often red and hot

Courtship

527. "clerk": at this time the scholars at Oxford were also in clerical orders and as such had to obey the rule of celibacy. Jenkin's marriage to the Wife would bring his scholarly career to a close.

THE WIFE OF BATH

[Lines 541-563]

For verray shame, and blamed hymself for he
For very shame, and he blamed himself that he

Had toold to me so greet a pryvetee.
Had told me such a great secret.

And so bifel that ones in a Lente—
And so it came about that once in Lent—

So often tymes I to my gossyb wente,
I often went to my girl friend's,

For evere yet I loved to be gay,   545
For I always loved to be gay,

And for to walke in March, Averill, and May,
And to walk in March, April, and May

From hous to hous, to heere sondry tales—
From house to house, to hear various tales—

That Jankyn clerk and my gossyb dame Alys
That Jenkin the clerk and my friend Dame Alice

And I myself into the feeldes wente.
And I myself went into the fields.

Myn housbonde was at Londoun al that Lente;   550
My husband was in London all that Lent;

I hadde the bettre leyser for to pleye,
I had more leisure to play,

And for to se, and eek for to be seye
And to see, and also to be seen

Of lusty folk. What wiste I wher my grace
By lively folk. What did I know where my favor

Was shapen for to be, or in what place?
Was destined to be bestowed, or in what place?

Therfore I made my visitacions   555
Therefore I made my appearances

To vigilies and to processions,
At vigils and at processions,

To prechyng eek, and to thise pilgrimages,
At preachings also, and pilgrimages like this,

To pleyes of myracles, and to mariages,
At miracle plays and at marriages,

And wered upon my gaye scarlet gytes.
And wore my gay scarlet gowns.

Thise wormes ne thise motthes ne this mytes,   560
The worms and moths and mites,

Upon my peril, frete hem never a deel;
I say it at my peril, ate them not a bit.

And wostow why? For they were used weel.
*And would you know why? Because they were well
    used.*

Now wol I tellen forth what happed me.
Now will I tell what happened to me.

The "Lusty People"

548. "Jankyn": diminutive of John, a conventional name for a clerk. "Alys": here interchangeable with Alisoun.

556. "vigilies": feasts on the eve of saints' days.

558. "pleyes of myracles": the miracle plays were religious dramas representing incidents in the lives of saints or martyrs; the term was loosely used for any kind of religious drama.

By the time of her marriage to Jenkin, Chaucer has made some subtle but significant changes in

THE WIFE OF BATH

[Lines 564-587]

the Wife. There had been no doubt of her beauty and power in her first three marriages, where she had been able to dominate her husbands either through sexual attraction or guile or sheer force.

By the time of her fourth marriage she is still, she says, "'yong and ful of ragerye," a word which may mean either wantonness or passion. She goes on to describe her delight in the pleasures of the senses. She "koude daunce to an harpe smale" and sing "as any nyghtyngale," particularly after "a draughte of sweete wyn!" She tells us that her thoughts turn "on Venus," and that her mouth is "likerous," a word which may mean either greedy or lecherous.

This special emphasis on sensual delight is placed here by Chaucer to imply the Wife's uneasy feeling that these pleasures will soon pass and that she, like all other things, must age. There is a note of something like desperation in recitation of her sensual appetite and sexual vigor. In the very next passage (469-79) we see her realization of the fact that time passes and pleasure fades. "Age, allas" has taken from her her "beautee" and her "pith."

In her aggressive assertion that she will still try to be merry there is just a touch of pathos, very like that we feel in Falstaff in Shakespeare's Henry IV, when he clings to the pleasures of the flesh in the face of oncoming age.

This is not to say that the Wife is to be pitied—she will always be far too powerfully alive for that. But it is Chaucer's way of suggesting that even she is sometimes aware of the fact that her own robust energy and love of life must fail.

She readily admits that she takes Jenkin "for love, and no richesse." The situation of her first three marriages is now reversed. He is the young and desirable partner (he is twenty to her forty), and she is the one with wealth.

However, Chaucer does not develop this theme of the Wife's aging too far, since it would upset the picture he wants to give of her, and that picture—of a woman no longer young, but passionately indestructible—is the one that remains in our minds.

I seye that in the feeldes walked we,
I said that we were walking in the fields,

Til trewely we hadde swich daliance, 565
Until truly we had flirted so much,

This clerk and I, that of my purveiance
This clerk and I, that in my foresight

I spak to hym and seyde hym how that he,
I spoke to him and told him that he,

If I were wydwe, sholde wedde me.
If I were a widow, could marry me.

For certeinly, I sey for bobance,
Certainly, I do not say as a boast,

Yet was I nevere withouten purveiance 570
I was never yet without foresight

Of mariage n' of othere thynges eek.
Concerning marriage, nor of other things.

I holde a mouses herte nat worth a leek
I hold a mouse's life not worth a leek

That hath but oon hole for to sterte to,
That has but one hole to run to,

And if that faille, thanne is al ydo.
And if that fails, then it is all finished.

I bar hym on honde he hadde enchanted me 575
I made him believe he had enchanted me

(My dame taughte me that subtiltee);
(My mother taught me that trick);

And eek I seyde I mette of hym al nyght,
And I told him I dreamed of him all night,

He wolde han slayn me as I lay upright,
That he would have slain me as I lay on my back,

And al my bed was ful of verray blood—
And that my bed was full of blood—

'But yet I hope that ye shal do me good; 580
'But yet I hope that you shall do me good;

For blood bitokeneth gold, as me was taught.'
For blood means gold, as I was taught.'

And al was fals; I dremed of it right naught,
And it was a lie; I dreamed no such thing,

But as I folwed ay my dames loore,
But I was following my mother's teaching,

As wel of that as of othere thynges moore.
As well here as in many other things.

But now sire—lat me se, what shal I seyn? 585
But now sir—let me see, what was I saying?

Aha, by God, I have my tale ageyn.
Aha, by God, I recall my story again.

Whan that my fourthe housbonde was on beere,
When my fourth husband was on his bier,

572. "leek": small vegetable resembling an onion.

581. "blood bitokeneth gold": this was common doctrine in the interpretation of dreams—both were red and both were precious.

THE WIFE OF BATH

[Lines 588-611]

Venus

It is true that Chaucer's characters are universal: we can imagine a Host, a Miller, or a Wife of Bath existing today — with some obvious alterations — as well as in the fourteenth century. But we must also recall that they were conceived in the fourteenth cen-

I weep algate, and made sory cheere,
I wept continually, and was of sad appearance,

As wyves mooten, for it is usage,
As wives must, for it is customary,

And with my coverchief covered my visage;   590
And with my kerchief covered my face;

But for that I was purveyed of a make,
But since I was provided with a mate,

I wepte but smal, and that I undertake.
I wept but little, I can tell you.

To chirche was myn housbonde born amorwe
My husband was borne to church in the morning

With neighebores that for hym maden sorwe;
By neighbors who mourned for him;

And Jankyn oure clerk was oon of tho.   595
And Jenkin our clerk was one of them.

As help me God, whan that I saw hym go
So help me God, when I watched him walk

After the beere, me thoughte he hadde a paire
After the bier, I thought he had a pair

Of legges and of feet so clene and faire
Of legs and feet so clean cut and fair

That al myn herte I yaf unto his hoold.
That all my heart I gave to him.

He was, I trowe, twenty wynter oold,   600
He was, I think, twenty winters old,

And I was fourty, if I shal seye sooth;
And I was forty, if I speak the truth;

But yet I hadde alwey a coltes tooth.
But yet I always had a colt's tooth.

Gat-tothed I was, and that bicam me weel;
I was gap-toothed, and that became me well;

I hadde the prente of Seint Venus seel.
I had the birthmark of Saint Venus' seal.

As help me God, I was a lusty oon,   605
May God help me, I was a lusty one,

And faire, and riche, and yong, and wel bigoon,
And fair, and rich, and young, and well provided for,

And trewely, as myne housbondes tolde me,
And truly, as my husbands told me,

I hadde the beste *quonyam* myghte be.
I had the best pudendum there could be.

For certes, I am al Venerien
For certainly, I am entirely Venerian

In feelyng, and myn herte is Marcien.   610
In feeling, and my heart is Martian.

Venus me yaf my lust, my likerousnesse,
Venus gave me my lust, my lecherousness,

602. "coltes tooth": "tooth" frequently signified taste, and here the meaning is youthful and ardent appetite.
603. "gat-toothed": this feature was supposed to indicate a bold and lascivious nature.
604. "Seint Venus": the goddess of love was sometimes sanctified in this way, usually ironically.

THE WIFE OF BATH

[Lines 612-635]

tury, when notions of human behavior and motivation were vastly different from our own.

The passage in which the Wife discusses the influence on her of the planets Mars and Venus is a good example of this difference. What we today loosely call the "behavorial sciences" would, for the medieval thinker, have been reducible to the study of the influence on man of humors, alchemical elements, and the planets.

We may hold no brief for such medieval "sciences" as alchemy, astrology, or chiromancy, but there objective truth does not matter. What matters is that in Chaucer's day they were taken very seriously, and therefore they have a significant bearing on the construction of a literary character.

As W. C. Curry has said: "The medieval sciences, however ludicrously inadequate they now seem to have been, were doubtless as important to the people of the fourteenth century as accepted principles of today are to us—and as powerful in helping to shape and mould character. Hence they must have exerted no little influence on the formation of Chaucer's ideas."

The Wife of Bath goes into some detail concerning the astrological aspect of her character. She has the "prente of Seint Venus," making her lusty, and that of Mars, providing "hardynesse." Her zodiacal sign is "Taur and Mars ther inne" which would, to the medieval reader, imply a great deal more than Chaucer explicitly says about her.

In his book Chaucer and the Medieval Sciences, Prof. Curry gives some of the medieval opinions of those born under Taurus, with the conjunction of the influences of Mars and Venus. Here are some excerpts: "He that has Mars in his ascendants shall be exposed to many dangers, and commonly at last receives a great scar in his face. When Mars is Lord of a Woman's Ascendant, and Venus is posited in it, or Venus Lady of it, and Mars in it, 'tis more than probable that she will Cuckold her husband." "Mars and Venus denote the Wife full of spirit, movable, an ill Housewife,

And Mars yaf me my sturdy hardynesse;
And Mars gave me my sturdy boldness;

Myn ascendent was Taur and Mars ther inne—
My astrological sign was Mars in Taurus—

Allas, allas, that evere love was synne!
Alas, alas, that ever love was sin!

I folwed ay myn inclinacion   615
I always followed my inclination;

By vertu of my constellacion;
By virtue of my constellation;

That made me I koude noght withdrawe
That made me so that I could not withhold

My chambre of Venus from a good felawe.
My chamber of Venus from a good fellow.

Yet have I Martes mark upon my face,
Yet I have the mark of Mars upon my face,

And also in another privee place.   620
And also in another private place.

For God so wys be my savacion,
For God in his wisdom be my salvation,

I loved nevere by no discrecion,
I never loved with any discretion,

But evere folwede myn appetit,
But always followed my appetite,

Al were he short on long or blak or whit;
Whether he were short or tall or dark or light;

I took no kepe, so that he liked me,   625
I took no heed, as long as he pleased me,

How poore he was, ne eek of what degree.
How poor he was, nor of what rank either.

What sholde I seye but at the monthes ende,
What can I say, but at the month's end,

This joly clerk Jankyn that was so hende
This handsome clerk Jenkin that was so pleasant

Hath wedded me with greet solempnytee;
Married me with great ceremony;

And to him yaf I al the lond and fee   630
And I gave him all the land and property

That evere was me yeven therbifore—
That had ever been given to me before—

But afterward repented me ful sore;
But afterward repented sorely;

He nolde suffre no thyng of my list.
He would not allow any of my wishes.

By God, he smoot me ones on the lyst,
By God, he hit me once on the ear,

For that I rente out of his book a leef,   635
Because I tore a page out of his book,

613. "Myn ascendent....": astrologically, the Wife's birth occurred when the zodiacal sign of Taurus was rising over the horizon. Taurus was called the mansion of Venus, and the appearance of Mars shows the influence of that planet. See Commentary.

616. "By vertu....": controlled by the position of planets at birth.

Mars

THE WIFE OF BATH

[Lines 636-659]

prodigall, and that she is or will be an Adulterer." "The person born when Mars is in conjunction with Venus has a complexion pleasingly red mixed with white; a face rounded but not too full with cheeks appropriately plump; lovely eyes a little too dark for greatest beauty but not black enough to be called ugly; and a body not fat to the point of being obese, but, as one might say, semi-fat."

The Wife, Prof. Curry continues, is the embodiment of the conflicting influences of Mars and Venus. It is the influence of Venus which makes her both desirable and desiring; that of Mars which impels her to gain, at all costs, domination over her husbands.

He sums up the view the medieval reader, knowing the Wife's horoscope, would have of her: "Instead of having the naturally beautiful and well-proportioned figure which might have been hers under the free, beneficent influence of Venus, she is endowed by the Mars-Venus combination with a stockily built, ungraceful buxom form of medium height. The strength which should have accompanied grace and beauty has been distorted into a powerful fecund energy; her large hips indicate excessive virility. ... Mars has given her a slightly heavy face inclined to fatness, characterized perhaps by coarsened features and certainly by a florid complexion, which indicates that the woman is immodest, loquacious, and given to drunkenness. ... The vice is strident and raised continually in indelicate jest and vulgar banter. Such a voice is significant in its betrayal of the Wife's voluptuous and luxurious nature; one suspects that she knows only too well how to 'laughe and carpe' in fellowship with the most dissolute rakes among the pilgrims...."

The influence of Venus makes its subject "tender-hearted, bountiful and pleasure-loving." But this influence is somewhat distorted in the Wife by the presence of Mars. "The temperament which might have been hers has been cheapened by Mars, so that she flashily decks herself out in gaudy colours —in scarlet dresses and hose, to say nothing of brand new shoes

That of the strook myn ere wax al deef.
So that my ear became entirely deaf from the blow.

Stibourne I was as is a leonesse,
I was as stubborn as a lioness,

And of my tonge a verray jangleresse,
And with my tongue a real chatterer,

And walke I wolde, as I had doon biforn,
And I would walk, as I had done before,

From hous to hous, although he had it sworn;   640
From house to house, although he had forbidden it;

For which he often tymes wolde preche,
And for this he would often preach,

And me of olde Romayn gestes teche;
And teach me ancient Roman stories;

How he Symplicius Gallus lefte his wif,
How Simplicius Gallus left his wife

And hire forsook for terme of al his lif,
And forsook her for the rest of his life,

Noght but for open-heveded he hir say   645
For nothing but that he saw her bareheaded

Lokyng out at his dore upon a day.
Looking out of his door one day.

Another Romayn tolde he me by name,
Another Roman he named to me,

That, for his wyf was at a someres game
That, because his wife attended a summer's game

Withouten his wityng, he forsook hire eke.
Without his knowledge, he forsook her too.

And thanne wolde he upon his Bible seke   650
And then he would look up in his Bible

That ilke proverbe of Ecclesiaste
That proverb in Ecclesiastes

Where he comandeth and forbedeth faste
Where he commands and strictly forbids

Man shal nat suffre his wyf go roule aboute.
Man shall not allow his wife to roam about.

Thanne wolde he seye right thus withouten doute:
Then would he say this, without any doubt:

'Whoso that buyldeth his hous al of salwes,   655
'Whoso builds his house entirely of twigs,

And priketh his blynde hors over the falwes,
And rides his blind horse over ditches,

And suffreth his wyf to go seken halwes,
And allows his wife to go visiting shrines,

Is worthy to been hanged on the galwes!'
Is worthy to hang on the gallows!'

But al for noght, I sette noght an hawe
But all for nothing, I did not care a berry

Milkmaid and Beggar

647. "Another Romayn": P. Sempronius Sophus, whose story occurs in the volume of stories mentioned at 642.

648. "someres game": the games and revels on Midsummer's Eve. The husband cited here is not to be blamed, since these games were far from innocent, but this would doubtless recommend them to the Wife of Bath.

650. "he": Jenkin.

652. "he": the writer of Ecclesiastes.

THE WIFE OF BATH

[Lines 660-683]

and silver spurs—and adorns herself on Sundays with a coverchief weighing ten pounds and on the pilgrimage with a hat as large as a buckler. . . . But worst of all, Mars has played havoc with the luxurious impulses — the 'likerousnesse'—which come from Venus; she has always had a 'coltes tooth.' Whatever else she may be, in the Prologue to her tale she appears an unusually healthy and frank female animal, human and sexually attractive, whose dominating idea seems to be the glorification of fleshly delights and the gratification of physical desire."

We have already noted that the book from which Jenkin reads, and which brings about the final outburst of hostilities between himself and his wife, is an anthology

Of his proverbes n' of his olde sawe;   660
For his proverbs or his old saws;

Ne I wolde nat of hym corrected be.
Nor would I be corrected by him.

I hate hym that my vices telleth me,
I hate him who tells me of my vices,

And so doo mo, God woot, of us than I.
And so do more of us, God knows, than I.

This made hym with me wood al outrely;
This made him furious with me;

I nolde noght forbere hym in no cas.   665
I could not let him alone in any case.

   Now wol I seye yow sooth, by Seint Thomas,
   Now I will tell you the truth, by Saint Thomas,

Why that I rente out of his book a leef,
As to why I tore a page out of his book,

For which he smoot me so that I was deef.
For which he hit me so hard I became deaf.

He hadde a book that gladly, nyght and day,
He had a book that happily, night and day,

For his disport he wolde rede alway;   670
He read continually for his entertainment.

He cleped it Valerie and Theofraste,
He called it Valerius and Theophrastus,

At which book he lough alwey ful faste.
At which book he always laughed uproariously.

And eek ther was somtyme a clerk at Rome,
And besides there was once a clerk at Rome,

A cardinal, that highte Seint Jerome,
A cardinal called Saint Jerome,

That made a book agayn Jovinian;   675
Who wrote a book against Jovinian;

In which book eek ther was Tertulan,
In which book there was also Tertullian,

Crysippus, Trotula, and Helowys,
Chrysippus, Trotula, and Heloise,

That was abbesse nat fer fro Parys;
Who was an abbess not far from Paris;

And eek the Parables of Salomon,
And also the Proverbs of Solomon,

Ovides Art, and bookes many oon—   680
Ovid's Art, and many another book—

And alle thise were bounden in o volume.
And all these were bound in one volume,

And every nyght and day was his custume,
And every night and day as was his custom,

Whan he hadde leyser and vacacion
When he had leisure and spare time

671. "Valerie and Theofraste": this refers to an anthology of some of the best-known medieval satires on women and marriage.

676. Tertullian was the author of several treatises in which chastity is exalted above marriage.

677. Chrysippus is mentioned in Jerome's Epistle.
Trotula was held to be a woman physician, author of a work on female ailments.
Heloise was secretly married to the great scholar, Abelard. She spent her last years in a convent, of which she became prioress.

680. "Ovides Art": The Latin poet Ovid's Ars Amatoria (Art of Love).

THE WIFE OF BATH

[Lines 684-707]

of anti-feminist anecdotes and represents a medieval literary form of long standing. Certainly it offers an abundance of evidence against "wikked wyves" — beginning with Eve ("That womman was the los of al mankynde") and running through the tales of Samson, Hercules, Clytemnestra, Pasiphae, and all the rest of the traditional figures used in the medieval attack on woman.

The incidents related are in themselves horrifying enough, but the exaggeration with which the Wife babbles them out takes the tragic sting out of them.

We can hardly fail to see the ironic humor in the story of Lucilia, who loved her husband with such ardor that she gave him an overdose of love-potion, thereby doing away with him entirely.

The vignette of the philosopher Socrates whose wife, before she had finished berating him verbally, emptied a chamber pot over his head, is a good example of Chaucer's dry wit. What could be more philosophical than his calm observation that before the thunder ends the rain is liable to begin?

The long recital of feminine delinquency has another, literary, purpose. One of the most powerful literary traditions of the Middle Ages was the celebration of what is usually called "courtly love." According to this tradition the lover is obliged to worship his "mistress" as though she were a diety. He sacrifices himself to her, and her every whim is his command.

It has been pointed out that this attitude would arise quite naturally in the Middle Ages, when obligation and service to one's lord was regarded as the basis of all society; in fact the doctrine of courtly love has been called the "feudalization of love."

However that may be, the doctrine produced an immense amount of literature, both in prose and poetry, in which women were exalted as angelic beings, incapable of any of the natural human failings. Chaucer himself had written a good deal in this vein, and in his translation of the first part of the Roman de la Rose had

From oother worldly occupacion,
From other worldly occupations,

To reden in this book of wikked wyves.   685
To read this book of wicked women.

He knew of hem mo legendes and lyves
He knew more legends and biographies of them

Than been of goode wyves in the Bible.
Than there are of good women in the Bible.

For trusteth wel, it is an impossible
For believe it, it is an impossibility

That any clerk wol speke good of wyves,
For any clerk to speak well of women,

But if it be of holy seintes lyves,   690
Except for the lives of holy saints,

Ne of noon oother womman never the mo.
Never of any woman.

Who peynted the leon, tel me who?
Who painted the lion, tell me who?

By God, if wommen hadde writen stories,
By God, if women had written the stories,

As clerkes han withinne hir oratories,
As clerks have in their oratories,

They wolde han writen of men moore wikkednesse   695
They would have written more evil of men

Than al the mark of Adam may redresse.
Than all the race of Adam can redress.

The children of Mercurie and of Venus
The children of Mercury and of Venus

Been in hir wirkyng ful contrarius;
Work in quite contrary ways;

Mercurie loveth wysdam and science,
Mercury loves wisdom and knowledge,

And Venus loveth riot and dispence;   700
And Venus loves revelry and lavishness;

And for hir diverse disposicion,
And because of their different temperaments,

Ech falleth in otheres exaltacion.
Each is low when the other is exalted.

And thus, God woot, Mercurie is desolat
And thus, God knows, Mercury is powerless

In Pisces, wher Venus is exaltat;
In Pisces, where Venus is exalted;

And Venus falleth ther Mercurie is reysed;   705
And Venus falls where Mercury is raised;

Therfore no womman of no clerk is preysed.
Therefore no woman is praised by any clerk.

The clerk, whan he is old and may noght do
The clerk, when he is old and cannot do

692. The reference is to Aesop's fable of the lion who looked at the painting of a hunter slaying a lion, and said, "Yes, but who painted the picture? A lion might have done it differently." The Wife is suggesting that if women wrote books instead of clerics, they would be anticlerical instead of anti-feminine.

694. "oratories": small chapels or studies, for private prayers.

697-706. The planet Mercury favors scholars, and Venus lovers. Mercury at its highest point (exaltation) coincides with Venus at its lowest (dejection) and vice versa; therefore their human representatives, scholars and women, can never agree.

46

THE WIFE OF BATH

[Lines 708-731]

put into English one of the outstanding examples of the form.

Any dominant literary fashion
usually produces a counter-fashion,
and the reaction against the literature of courtly love produced the
kind of writing that Chaucer is
doing in the "Jenkin's book" passage. Far from being an angel, a
fair woman is no better than "a
gold ring in a sowes nose."

Cupid and Psyche

Of Venus werkes worth his olde sho,
The works of Venus worth his old shoe,

Thanne sit he doun and writ in his dotage
Then he sits down and writes in his dotage

That wommen kan nat kepe hir mariage!　　710
That women cannot be faithful in marriage!

But now to purpos why I tolde thee
But now to the reason why as I told you

That I was beten for a book, pardee!
I was beaten for a book, by heaven!

Upon a nyght Jankyn, that was oure sire,
One night Jenkin, that was my husband,

Redde on his book, as he sat by the fire,
Read in his book, as he sat by the fire,

Of Eva first, that for hir wikkednesse　　715
First of Eve, because of her wickedness

Was al mankynde broght to wrecchednesse
All mankind was brought to wretchedness,

For which that Jhesu Crist hymself was slayn,
For which Jesus Christ himself was slain,

That boghte us with his herte blood agayn.
Who redeemed us again with his heart's blood.

Lo, heere expres of wommen may ye fynde,
Lo, here you may read expressly about woman,

That womman was the los of al mankynde.　　720
That woman was the downfall of all mankind.

Tho redde he me how Sampson loste his heres:
Then he read me how Samson lost his hair:

Slepynge, his lemman kitte it with hir sheres;
Sleeping, his lover cut it with her shears;

Thurgh which treson loste he bothe his eyen.
Through which betrayal he lost both his eyes.

Tho redde he me, if that I shal nat lyen,
Then he read me, unless I lie,

Of Hercules and of his Dianyre,　　725
Of Hercules and of his Deianeira,

That caused hym to sette hymself afyre.
Who caused him to set himself on fire.

No thyng forgat he the care and the wo
By no means did he forget the sorrow and woe

That Socrates hadde with his wyves two;
That Socrates had with his two wives;

How Xantippa caste pisse upon his heed.
How Xantippe emptied a piss-pot on his head.

This sely man sat stille as he were deed;　　730
The poor man sat still, as though dead;

He wiped his heed, namoore dorste he seyn
He wiped his head, no more dared he say

725. Deianeira, fearing to lose Hercules, sent him a shirt which she had
dipped in what she thought was a
love potion, made of the blood of
the centaur, Nessus. Hercules had
himself shot Nessus and was tortured by the poison which his own
arrow had introduced into Nessus'
blood. The pain was so great that
he threw himself upon a fire to
end it.

729. Xantippe, Socrates' wife, was a
legendary scold.

But 'Er that thonder stynte, comth a reyn.'
But 'Before the thunder stops, the rain comes.'

Of Phasipha that was the queene of Crete,
Of Pasiphae who was the queen of Crete,

For shrewednesse hym thoughte the tale swete;
For malice, he thought the tale was sweet;

Fy, speke namore—it is a grisly thyng—   735
Fie, say no more—it was a grisly thing—

Of hire horrible lust and hir likyng.
Of her horrible lust and her choice.

Of Clitermystra for hir lecherye
Of Clytemnestra, was lechery

That falsly made hir housbonde for to dye,
Caused the treacherous death of her husband,

He redde it with ful good devocion.
He read that with great devotion.

He tolde me eek for what occasion   740
He also told me the reason

Amphiorax at Thebes loste his lyf.
Amphiaraus lost his life at Thebes.

Myn housbonde hadde a legende of his wyf
My husband had a legend about his wife

Eriphilem, that for an ouche of gold
Ariphyle, who for an ornament of gold

Hath prively unto the Grekes told
Secretly told the Greeks

Wher that hir housbonde hidde hym in a place,   745
The place where her husband had hidden himself,

For which he hadde at Thebes sory grace.
Because of which he had a sad fate at Thebes.

Of Lyvia tolde he me and of Lucye:
Of Livia he told me and of Lucilia:

They bothe made hir housbondes for to dye,
They both caused their husbands to die,

That oon for love, that oother was for hate.
One for love, the other out of hate;

Lyvia hir housbonde, on an even late,   750
Livia her husband, late one evening,

Empoysoned hath, for that she was his fo;
Poisoned, because she was his foe.

Lucia, likerous, loved hir housbonde so
Lucilia, lecherous, loved her husband so

That, for he sholde alwey upon hire thynke,
That, so that he would always think of her,

She yaf hym swich a manere love-drynke
She gave him a love potion of such a sort

That he was deed er it were by the morwe.   755
That he was dead before next morning.

732. By "thunder" here Socrates means Xantippe's voice.

733. Pasiphae: Ovid, in Ars Amatoria recounts how Minos, King of Crete, had a wife who loved a bull; from their union came the Minotaur.

737. Clytemnestra was the wife of Agamemnon, the Greek leader in the Trojan War. While he was absent she fell in love with Aegisthus, and the two murdered Agamemnon on his return.

741. Amphiaraus allowed himself to be persuaded to join an expedition against Thebes, although he knew it would mean his death. He was swallowed up in an earthquake.

747. Livia murdered her husband, Drusus, at the bidding of her lover, Sejanus.
Lucilia was the wife of the poet Lucretius.

And thus algates housbondes han sorwe.
And thus husbands always have sorrow.

Thanne tolde he me how oon Latumyus
Then he told me how one Latumius

Compleyned unto his felawe Arrius
Complained to his friend Arrius

That in his gardyn growed swich a tree,
That in his garden grew a certain tree

On which he seyde how that his wyves thre   760
On which he said that his three wives

Hanged hemself for herte despitus.
Hanged themselves out of spite.

'O leeve brother,' quod this Arrius,
'O dear brother,' said this Arrius,

'Yif me a plante of thilke blessed tree,
'Give me a cutting of this blessed tree,

And in my gardyn planted shal it be.'
And it shall be planted in my garden.'

Of latter date of wyves hath he red   765
He read of wives of later date

That somme han slayn hir housbondes in hir bed
Of whom some had slain their husbands in their beds

And lete hir lechour dighte hire al the nyght,
And let their lovers sleep with them all night,

Whan that the corps lay in the floor upright;
While the corpse lay supine on the floor;

And somme han dryven nayles in hir brayn
And some had driven nails into their brains

Whil that they slepte, and thus they han hem slayn;   770
While they slept, and so killed them;

Somme han hem yeven poysoun in hir drynke;
Some gave them poison in their drinks;

He spak moore harm than herte may bithynke;
He spoke more wickedness than the mind can think;

And therwithal he knew of mo proverbes
And in addition, he knew more proverbs

Than in this world ther growen gras or herbes.
Than there grow grass and plants in this world.

'Bet is,' quod he, 'thyn habitacioun   775
'It is better,' he said, 'to live

Be with a leon or a foul dragoun,
With a lion or a foul dragon,

Than with a womman usyng for to chide.'
Than with a woman who scolds.'

'Bet is,' quod he, 'hye in the roof abyde,
'It is better,' he said, 'to dwell on the roof,

Than with an angry wyf doun in the hous;
Than down in the house with an angry wife;

757. The story of the tree upon which wives might be expected to hang themselves was a medieval favorite and appears in several versions.

Feeding Hogs Acorns

THE WIFE OF BATH

[Lines 780-803]

The battle between Jenkin and the Wife is vividly and dramatically told. It is characteristic of the Wife (and perhaps a result of her "Martian" influence) that she is the aggressor, tearing the pages from the book and knocking her husband into the fire; it is even more characteristic that, pretending she is dying from his blow and asking for a last kiss, she tricks him to come near enough so that she can hit him again.

The purpose of the fight is to point up the moral with which the Wife began her long prologue: that marriages will be happy when the wife has the "maistrye, al the soveraynetee." The Wife will present this same thesis, in somewhat different form, in her tale.

They been so wikked and contrarious, 780
They are so wicked and contrary,

They haten that hir housbondes loven ay.'
They always hate that which their husbands love.'

He seyde, 'A womman cast hir shame away
He said, 'A woman casts her shame away

Whan she cast of hir smok,' and forthermo,
When she casts off her smock,' and furthermore,

'A fair womman, but she be chaast also,
'A fair woman, unless she be chaste as well,

Is lyk a gold ryng in a sowes nose.' 785
Is like a gold ring in a sow's nose.'

Who wolde wene, or who wolde suppose
Who can understand, or who could imagine,

The wo that in myn herte was and pyne?
The grief and torment that was in my heart?

And whan I saugh he wolde nevere fyne
And when I saw that he would never stop

To reden on this cursed book al nyght,
Reading in his cursed book all night,

Al sodeynly thre leves have I plyght 790
Suddenly I tore three leaves

Out of his book right as he radde, and eke
Out of his book right while he was reading, and also

I with my fist so took hym on the cheke
I so struck him with my fist on the cheek

That in oure fyr he fil bakward adoun.
That he fell down backward in our fire.

And he up stirte as dooth a wood leoun,
And up he jumped like an enraged lion,

And with his fest he smoot me on the heed 795
And with his fist he hit me on the head

That in the floor I lay as I were deed.
So that on the floor I lie as though I were dead.

And whan he saugh how stille that I lay,
And when he saw how still I lay,

He was agast, and wolde han fled his way,
He was aghast, and would have run away,

Til atte laste out of my swogh I brayde.
Until at last I awoke from my swoon.

'O hastow slayn me, false theef?' I sayde, 800
'O have you killed me, false thief?' I said

'And for my land thus hastow mordred me?
'And have you murdered me thus for my land?

Er I be deed, yet wol I kiss thee.'
Yet before I die I would kiss you.'

And neer he cam and kneled faire adoun,
And he came near, and kneeled gently down,

Astrolabe

THE WIFE OF BATH

[Lines 804–826]

And seyde, 'Deere suster Alisoun,
And said, 'Dear sister Alison,

As help me God, I shal thee nevere smyte.　805
So help me God, I shall never strike you.

That I have doon, it is thyself to wyte.
For what I have done, you are to blame.

Foryeve it me, and that I thee biseke.'
Forgive me for it, I beseech you.'

And yet eftsoones I hitte hym on the cheke,
And yet again I hit him on the cheek,

And seyde, 'Theef, thus muchel am I wreke;
And said, 'Thief, that much I am revenged;

Now wol I dye; I may no lenger speke.'　810
Now I will die, I can no longer speak.'

But at the laste, with muchel care and wo,
But at last, with much effort and grief,

We fille acorded by us selven two.
We reached an agreement between ourselves.

He yaf me al the bridel in myn hond,
He gave all authority into my hand,

To han the governance of hous and lond,
To direct the house and property,

And of his tonge and of his hond also;　815
And his tongue and hand also;

And made hym brenne his book anon right tho.
And I made him burn his book at once, right there.

And whan that I hadde geten unto me,
And when I had gained for myself,

By maistrye, al the soveraynetee,
By skill, the complete sovereignty,

And that he seyde, 'Myn owene trewe wyf,
And he had said, 'My own true wife,

Do as thee lust the terme of al thy lyf;　820
Do as you please all the rest of your life;

Keep thyn honour, and keep eek myn estaat,'
*Have charge of your honor, and keep my estate as
　well,'*

After that day we hadden never debaat.
After that day we never had any strife.

God help me so, I was to hym as kynde
God help me, I was as kind to him

As any wyf from Denmark unto Inde,
As any wife from Denmark to India,

And also trewe, and so was he to me.　825
And faithful as well, and so was he to me.

I pray to God that sit in magestee,
I pray to God who sits in majesty,

We have already seen, in connection with the Pardoner's interruption, the way in which Chaucer occasionally reminds us of the setting of these tales—the group of pilgrims who tell them and who, from time to time, wrangle among themselves. The sharp exchange between the Friar and the Summoner serves this purpose, as well as providing a contrast to what

Ewer

804. "suster": sometimes used as a general term of endearment.

815. "tonge . . . hond": i.e., control over his word and deed.

THE WIFE OF BATH

[Lines 827-850]

has been a very lengthy piece of narration. Again, as with the Pardoner, Chaucer adds to the dramatic interest of his work by revealing something of the personalities of his pilgrims.

The General Prologue has already introduced the Friar and the Summoner, and given us reason to think that there may be some contention between them. In medieval society they would be natural enemies, since they both prey on the same victim: the medieval peasant.

The Friar was a member of a begging order which had, in Chaucer's time, amassed a great deal of wealth. This Friar lives well and dresses well, but his personal profit is made by misusing his religious office and issuing easy absolution for a price.

The Summoner's function was to bring those who were accused of sinning to the ecclesiastical court; he was thus ideally placed for bribery and extortion, and Chaucer makes clear that he used his position accordingly.

Of the two, the Friar comes off best in the General Prologue. While he is dishonest, he is also likable, with a gift for merriment. The Summoner gets much harsher treatment. He is "lecherous as a sparwe" and much more blatant in using his clerical office for his own gain. For him a man's soul is in his purse.

The distinction between the two is subtly present in their brief argument. The Friar's opening is amiable enough (829); he simply draws attention, with a laugh, to what every listener must have been thinking: that the Wife's introduction to her tale was indeed a lengthy one. The Summoner then attacks him with real personal venom, out of all proportion to the offense—friars are forever interfering, they are like flies, in every dish, let them shut up and sit down!

Chaucer slyly underlines his point by making the Summoner complain that the Friar's "patience is gon," when it is clear that it is he himself who is enraged. Finally, of course, Chaucer means this ex-

---

So blesse his soule for his mercy deere.
To bless his soul out of his dear mercy.

Now wol I seye my tale, if ye wol heere."
Now I will tell my tale, if you will listen."

The Frere lough whan he hadde herd al this;
The friar laughed when he had heard all this;

"Now dame," quod he, "so have I joye or blis,   830
"Now madam," said he, "as I may have joy or bliss,

This is a long preamble of a tale."
This is a long preamble to a tale."

And whan the Somnour herde the Frere gale,
And when the Summoner heard the Friar speak out,

"Lo," quod the Somnour, "Goddes armes two!
"Lo," said the Summoner, "by God's two arms!

A frere wol entremette him everemo!
A friar will interfere every time!

Lo, goode men, a flye and eek a frere   835
Lo, good men, a fly and also a friar

Wol falle in every dyssh and eek matere.
Will fall into every dish and subject too.

What spekestow of preambulacioun?
Why do you speak of perambulation?

What, amble or trotte or pees or go sit doun!
What, amble or trot or keep still or go sit down!

Thou lettest oure disport in his manere."
You stop our pleasure in this way."

"Ye, woltow so, sire Somnour?" quod the Frere;   840
"Yes, will you so, sir Summoner?" said the Friar;

"Now by my feith, I shal, er that I go,
"Now by my faith, I shall, before I go,

Telle of a somnour swich a tale or two
Tell of a summoner such a tale or two

That al the folk shal laughen in this place."
That all the folk here will laugh."

"Now elles, Frere, I bishrewe thy face,"
"Now besides, Friar, I curse your face,"

Quod this Somnour, "and I bishrewe me,   845
Said this Summoner, "and I curse myself,

But if I telle tales two or thre
If I don't tell two or three tales

Of freres, er I come to Sidyngborne,
Of friars, before I get to Sittingbourne,

That I shal make thyn herte for to morne,
So I shall make your spirit grieve,

For wel I woot thy pacience is gon."
For I know well your patience is gone."

Oure Hooste cride, "Pees, and that anon!"   850
Our host cried, "Quiet, and that at once!"

The Summoner

827. The first "his" refers to Jenkin, the second to God.

847. "Sidyngborne": about forty miles from London.

THE WIFE OF BATH

[Lines 851-869]

change to whet the reader's appetite for the tales which the two will tell against each other after the Wife's tale is finished.

And seyde, "Lat the womman telle hir tale.
And said, "Let the woman tell her tale.

Ye fare as folk that dronken ben of ale.
You behave like people that are drunk with ale.

Do, dame, tel forth youre tale, and that is best."
Do, madam, tell your tale, that is best."

"Al redy, sire," quod she, "right as yow lest,
"All ready, sir," said she, "just as you please,

If I have licence of this worthy Frere."   855
If I have the permission of this worthy Friar."

"Yis, dame," quod he, "tel forth, and I wol heere."
"Yes, madam," said he, "say on, and I will listen."

Heere endeth the Wyf of Bathe hir Prologe.
Here ends the Wife of Bath's Prologue

The Wife of Bath's Tale

Heere bigynneth the Tale of the Wyf of Bathe.
Here begins the Wife of Bath's Tale

The Wife opens her tale with an evocation of "th' olde dayes of the kyng Arthour," when the land was "'fulfild with fayerye." We must not imagine "fayerye" in terms of the tiny, gossamer-winged creations of Walt Disney or of Tinker Bell in Peter Pan.

The diminutive, female fairy of our day was an invention of the late sixteenth century. The medieval use of the word denotes something closer to "spirit," or pagan god, a legacy of pre-Christian folk religion and magic. Fairy spirits of this kind are very common in folk tales and legends, particularly those of Celtic origin; the Wife's tale probably originated in Welsh or Irish folklore.

The Wife's introduction also contains an explicit attack on clerics, particularly friars. This seems to be included for two reasons.

In the first place the Wife, as a somewhat amoral and instinctive character, prefers the older, pagan attitudes to the repressions she associates with the clergy. She may well be a good Christian, but her instincts are anticlerical. She would much prefer "the elf-queene, with hir joly compaignye" to the snooping, scolding clerics.

In th' olde dayes of the kyng Arthour,
In the old days of King Arthur,

Of which that Britons speken greet honour,
Whom Britons hold in great honor,

Al was this land fulfild of fayerye.
All this land was filled with fairies.

The elf-queene, with hir joly compaignye;   860
The elf-queen, with her lovely company,

Daunced ful ofte in many a grene mede.
Often danced in many a green meadow.

This was the olde opinion, as I rede;
This was the old belief, which I have read;

I speke of many hundred yeres ago.
I speak of many hundred years ago.

But now kan no man se none elves mo,
But now no man can see elves anymore,

For now the grete charitee and prayeres   865
For now the great charity and prayers

Of lymytours and othere holy freres,
Of limiters and other holy friars,

That serchen every lond and every streem,
That frequent every land and every stream,

As thikke as motes in the sonne-beem,
As thick as motes in a sunbeam,

Blessynge halles, chambres, kichenes, boures,
Blessing halls, chambers, kitchens, boudoirs,

Medieval King

859. "fayerye": the word signifies not only supernatural beings but also the state of enchantment or illusion. Chaucer uses the words fairy and elf indiscriminately when speaking of the "inhabitants of the land of enchantment," and they are of human size, not the diminutive fairies of later literature.

866. "lymytours": licensed to beg within certain limits.

THE WIFE OF BATH

[Lines 870-893]

Second, the Friar probably irritates her as a representative of all she dislikes in the priesthood. In the General Prologue the Friar was represented as "a wantowne and a merye," someone who knew "daliaunce and fair langage" and was familiar with the "wommen of the toun." He is, in fact, a hypocrite, although Chaucer makes him an engaging one.

But hypocrisy about appetite and its satisfaction is one thing no one could ever accuse the Wife of, and she resents it in others, particularly those clerics who set themselves up as examples of Christian virtue. Hence the acid irony in her lines about women now being able to go "saufly up and doun" without fear of anything—except, that is, the loss of their honor to some wandering friar.

The tale that the Wife of Bath tells is a very old one and has its origins in myth, legend, and folklore. It has certain elements common to most such tales: (1) they begin with some crime which must be expiated, here the rape of the maiden; (2) they involve a journey, or quest for something, here the answer to the queen's question; (3) they turn on some sort of irony, often a promise which must be fulfilled in an unexpected way, as here, where the old woman demands to marry the knight; (4) they often end in a magical transformation, here the old woman's metamorphosis into a fair maiden; (5) the natural and the supernatural occur together.

This particular story occurs in many forms and in many cultures. The English version is often called the story of the "loathly lady"— the repulsive old woman who is made beautiful. Basically it is the story that we know best as Beauty and the Beast: someone who is ugly is transformed by a kiss, or an act of love, or even acceptance, into their original, beautiful state.

Despite its apparent simplicity, the story is rich in meaning. The

---

Citees, burghes, castels, hye toures,   870
Cities, boroughs, castles, high towers,

Thropes, bernes, shipnes, dayeryes—
Villages, barns, stables, dairies—

This maketh that ther been no fayeryes.
This makes it that there are no fairies.

For ther as wont to walken was an elf,
For where an elf used to walk,

Ther walketh now the lymytour hymself,
There walks now the limiter himself,

In undermeles and in morwenynges,   875
In afternoons and mornings,

And seith his matyns and his holy thynges
And says his matins and his holy things

As he gooth in his lymytacioun.
As he goes round his limitation.

Wommen may go now saufly up and doun;
Women may now go safely up and down;

In every bussh or under every tree
In every bush or under every tree

Ther is noon oother incubus but he,   880
There is no other incubus but he,

And he ne wol doon hem but dishonour.
And he will not do them anything but dishonor.

And so bifel it that this kyng Arthour
And so it came about that this King Arthur

Hadde in his hous a lusty bacheler,
Had in his house a lusty young knight,

That on a day cam ridynge fro ryver.
Who one day came riding from the river.

And happed that, allone as she was born,   885
And it happened that, alone as she was born,

He saugh a myde walkynge hym biforn;
He saw a maid walking ahead of him;

Of which mayde anon, maugree hir heed,
Of which maid at once, despite her protests,

By verray force, he rafte hir hydenhed;
By main force he stole her maidenhead;

For which oppression was swich clamour
On account of which violation there was such clamor

And swich pursute unto the kyng Arthour,   890
And such petitioning of King Arthur,

That dampned was this knyght for to be deed,
That this knight was condemned to be executed,

But cours of lawe, and sholde han lost his heed—
By course of law, and would have lost his head—

Paraventure swich was the statut tho—
Since such was the law then—

---

877. "lymytacioun": the limits within which the friar was allowed to beg.

880. "incubus": a devil in the form of a male human being, held to seduce women while they slept. Here and in the next line the Wife is being ironic at the Friar's expense. See Commentary.

883. "bacheler": not properly a knight, but an aspirant for knighthood. However, the hero of the tale is called knight throughout.

Lady Rousing Game with Tabor

THE WIFE OF BATH

[Lines 894-917]

most basic meaning is that an act of love (as in Beauty and the Beast) or even respect and humility (as the knight's submission to the old woman here) can change reality or make what was repellent beautiful or reveal the real beauty hitherto unperceived.

One of the greatest versions of the story outside of folk legend occurs in Coleridge's Rime of the Ancient Mariner. When the Mariner blesses the repellent sea snakes —that is, shows his love for them —the curse of the albatross falls from him, and the reviving rains come.

We can get some notion of the powerful imaginative appeal the story has had by the wide variety of cultures in which it has occurred, and in each one of which it must have been spontaneously composed.

There are versions in Icelandic, Gaelic, Turkish, and even Sanskrit. There is a traveler's tale reported by Sir John Mandeville in the fourteenth century of a fair lady "of the Ile of Lango" who was turned into a dragon and condemned to retain this form "until the tyme that a Knyghte come, that is so hardy, that dar come to hir and kiss hir on the Mouth."

The Icelandic version concerns Helgi, King of the Danes, who was forced to go to bed with a hideous old woman whom he found transformed, at dawn, into a beautiful maiden.

There is even an African folk tale of a man turned into a crocodile, who was returned to his human form when his bride was induced to lick his face.

Any story that has occurred as many times and in as many different forms as this gives imaginative form to some basic human conception, however it may be interpreted.

But that the queene and othere ladyes mo
But that the queen and other ladies as well

So longe preyeden the kyng of grace,   895
So long begged the king for mercy,

Til he his lyf graunted in the place,
Until he there granted him his life,

And yaf hym to the queene, al at hir wille,
And gave him to the queen, at her disposal,

To chese wheither she wolde hym save or spille.
To choose whether she would save or kill him.

The queene thanked the kyng with al hir myght,
The queen thanked the king with all her might,

And after this thus spak she to the knyght,   900
And after this she spoke thus to the knight,

Whan that she saugh hir tyme upon a day:
When she saw an opportunity one day:

"Thou standest yet," quod she, "in swich array
"You still stand," she said, "in such a situation

That of thy lyf yet hastow no suretee.
That you have no guarantee of life.

I grante thee lyf, if thou kanst tellen me
I grant you life, if you can tell me

What thyng is it that womeen moost desiren.   905
What is the thing that women most desire.

Be war, and keep thy nekke-boon from iren!
Be wary, and keep your neckbone from the iron!

And if thow kanst nat tellen it anon,
And if you cannot tell it at once,

Yet shal I yeve thee leve for to gon
Yet I will give you leave to go

A twelf-month and a day, to secche and lere
A twelvemonth and a day, to seek and learn

An answere suffisant in this matere;   910
A satisfactory answer to this problem;

And suretee wol I han, er that thou pace,
And I will have a guarantee, before you leave,

Thy body for to yelden in this place."
That you will yield up your body in this place."

Wo was this knyght, and sorwefully he siketh;
The knight was sad, and sorrowful he sighed;

But what! he may nat do al as hym liketh,
What of it! he couldn't do just as he wanted,

And at the laste he chees hym for to wende,   915
And at the last he chose to journey forth,

And come agayn right at the yeres ende,
And return again just at the year's end,

With swich answere as God wolde hym purveye;
With whatever answer God might give him;

Helmet

And taketh his leve and wendeth forth his weye.
And he took his leave and went on his way.

    He seketh every hous and every place
    He sought in every house and every place

Where as he hopeth for to fynde grace,   920
Wherever he hoped to find help,

To lerne what thyng wommen loven moost;
To learn what thing women love most;

But he ne koude arryven in no coost
But he never came to any region

Wher as he myghte fynde in this mateere
Where he could find, on this subject,

Two creatures accordynge in-feere.
Two creatures agreeing together.

    Somme seyde wommen loven best richesse,   925
    Some said women loved wealth best,

Somme seyde honour, some seyde jolynesse,
Some said honor, some said beauty,

Somme riche array, somme seyden lust abedde,
Some fine clothes, some said lust abed,

And oftetyme to be wydwe and wedde.
And to be often widowed and married.

Somme seyde that oure hertes been moost esed
Some said that our spirits are most comforted

Whan that we been yflatered and yplesed—   930
When we are flattered and pleased—

He gooth ful ny the sothe, I wol nat lye.
That comes near the truth, I will not lie.

A man shal wynne us best with flaterye;
A man shall win us best with flattery;

And with attendance and with bisynesse
And with attendance and with diligence

Been we ylymed, bothe moore and lesse.
We are caught, both high and low.

    And somme seyen that we loven best   935
    And some said that we love best

For to be free, and do right as us lest,
To be free, and to do just as we please,

And that no man repreve us of oure vice,
And that no man reprove us for our vice,

But seye that we be wise and no thyng nyce.
But say that we are wise, and in no way foolish.

For trewely ther is noon of us alle,
For truly there is not one of us all,

If any wight wol clawe us on the galle,   940
If any man scratches us on a sore spot,

That we nyl kike for he seith us sooth.
Who will not kick because he tells the truth.

929. "oure": the Wife begins here to speak in her own person, and her digression goes on for some fifty lines. It is characteristic that she should allow herself this conversational detour and adds a contrast to straightforward narrative delivery.

Candlestick

Assay, and he shal fynde it that so dooth;
Try it, and who does will find out;

For, be we never so vicious withinne,
For be we never so wicked within,

We wol been holden wise and clene of synne.
We want to be considered wise, and pure of sin.

And somme seyn that greet delit han we   945
And some said that we take great delight

For to been holden stable, and eek secree,
In being considered reliable and discreet,

And in o purpos stedefastly to dwelle,
And able to hold steadfastly to one purpose,

And nat biwreye thyng that men us telle—
And not betray things that men tell us—

But that tale is nat worth a rake-stele.
But that notion is not worth a rake handle.

Pardee, we wommen konne no thyng hele;   950
Heavens! we women can conceal nothing;

Witnesse on Myda,—wol ye heere the tale?
Witness Midas—will you hear the tale?

Ovyde, amonges othere thynges smale,
Ovid, among other short writings,

Seyde Myda hadde, under his longe heres,
Said that Midas had, under his long hair,

Growynge upon his heed two asses eres,
Two ass's ears growing on his head,

The whiche vice he hidde, as he best myghte,   955
Which deformity he hid, as best he could,

Ful subtilly from every mannes sighte,
Most craftily from every man's sight,

That, save his wyf, ther wiste of it namo.
So that, except for his wife, no one knew of it.

He loved hire moost, and trusted hire also;
He loved her greatly, and trusted her as well;

He preyed hire that to no creature
He begged her that to no creature

She sholde tellen of his disfigure.   960
Would she tell of his disfigurement.

She swoor him, "Nay," for al this world to wynne,
She swore to him, "No," for all the world,

She nolde do that vileynye or synne,
She would not do that wickedness or sin,

To make hir housbonde han so foul a name.
To give her husband so foul a name.

She nolde nat telle it for hir owene shame.
She would not tell it because of her own shame.

But nathelees, hir thoughte that she dyde,   965
But nonetheless, she thought she would die,

951. "wol ye heere ... ?": another digression, again typical of the Wife. The story of Midas and his his ass's ears is taken from Ovid's Metamorphoses. There it is the barber who shares the king's secret.

Investiture of a Knight

THE WIFE OF BATH

[Lines 966-989]

That she so longe sholde a conseil hyde;
Keeping a secret for so long;

Hir thoughte it swal so soore aboute hir herte
She felt it pressed so sorely on her heart

That nedely som word hire moste asterte;
That some word, of necessity, would escape her;

And sith she dorste telle it to no man,
And since she dared tell it to no man,

Doun to a marys faste by she ran—   970
Down to a nearby marsh she ran—

Til she cam there, hir herte was afyre—
Until she reached it, her heart was afire—

And as a bitore bombleth in the myre,
And as a bittern booms in the mire,

She leyde hir mouth unto the water doun:
She laid her mouth down to the water:

"Biwrey me nat, thou water, with thy soun,"
"Betray me not, thou water, with thy sound,"

Quod she. "To thee I telle it and namo;   975
Said she. "To thee I tell it and no one else;

Myn housbonde hath longe asses erys two!
My husband has two long ass's ears!

Now is myn herte al hool, now is it oute.
Now is my heart all healed, now it is out.

I myghte no lenger kepe it, out of doute."
I could no longer contain it, without a doubt."

Heere may ye se, thogh we a tyme abyde,
Here you may see, though we wait some time,

Yet out it moot; we kan no conseil hyde.   980
Yet it must out; we cannot keep a secret.

The remenant of the tale if ye wol heere,
If you will hear the rest of the tale,

Redeth Ovyde, and ther ye may it leere.
Read Ovid, and you may learn it there.

This knyght of which my tale is specially,
This knight, whom my tale specially concerns,

Whan that he saugh he myghte nat come therby,
When he saw that he could not discover it,

This is to seye, what wommen loven moost,   985
That is to say, what women love most,

Withinne his brest ful sorweful was the goost.
Within his breast his spirit was most sorrowful.

But hoom he gooth, he myghte nat sojourne;
But he went home, he could not delay;

The day was come that homward moste he tourne.
The day had come when he must turn homeward.

And in his wey it happed hym to ryde
And on his way it happened that he rode

In English the theme of the "loathly lady" is treated by Gower in his Tale of Florent in *Confessio Amantis*, and also survives in various ballads, chiefly "The Marriage of Sir Gawaine" and "The Weddynge of Sir Gawen and Dame Ragnell."

These ballads are too long to quote here, but we can get some idea of the way in which Chaucer handled his materials by giving F. J. Child's synopsis of the first. "King Arthur, apparently some day after Christmas, had been encountered in the forest by a bold baron armed with a club, who offered him the choice of fighting or ransoming himself by coming

972. "bombleth": the "booming" noise made by the bittern was for a long time thought to be produced by the bird sticking his beak in the water and blowing—hence its aptness here, where the wife "leyde hir mouth unto the water doun."

982. In Ovid's ending, reeds grow from the spot and whenever the wind blows they rustle, whispering the king's secret.

Pilgrim Sign

THE WIFE OF BATH

[Lines 990-1012]

back on New Year's Day and bringing word what women most desire. Arthur puts this question in all quarters, and having collected many answers, in which, possibly, he had little confidence, he rides to keep his day. On the way he meets a frightfully ugly woman; she intimates that she can help him. Arthur promises her Gawain in marriage if she will, and she imparts to him the right answer. Arthur finds the baron waiting for him in the forest and presents first the answers which he had collected and written down. These are contemptuously rejected. Arthur then says that he met a lady on the moor, who had told him that a woman would have her will. The baron says that the misshapen lady on the moor was his sister and that he will burn her if he can get hold of her. Upon Arthur's return he tells his knights that he has a wife for one of them. When they see the bride they decline the match in vehement terms, all but Gawain, who is somehow led to waive 'a little foul sight and misliking.' He takes her in all her repulsiveness, and she turns into a beautiful young woman. She asks Gawain whether he will have her in this likeness by night only or only by day. Gawain leaves the choice to her, and this is all that is needed to keep her perpetually beautiful. For a stepmother had bewitched her to go on the wild moor in that fiendly shape until she should meet some knight who would let her have her own will. Her brother, under a like spell, was to challenge men either to fight with him at odds or to answer his hard questions" (English and Scottish Ballads).

This ballad, or something like it, was probably Chaucer's source, and we can see how he has edited and compressed the story in the interests of artistic effect.

Arthur and Gawain are made one, that is, the man who has to make the choice gets the reward. The usual folk-tale alternative offered to the knight — "foul by night and fair by day or vice versa"—is changed to foul and faithful or fair and fickle, a much more complicated and demanding choice.

Finally, Chaucer makes the story one of suspense, since we do not

In al this care under a forest syde,   990
In all this worry, under a forest's edge,

Wher as he saugh upon a daunce go
Where he saw dancing

Of ladyes foure and twenty and yet mo;
Four and twenty ladies and yet more;

Toward the whiche daunce he drow ful yerne,
Toward which dance he drew most eagerly,

In hope that som wysdom sholde he lerne.
Hoping that he might learn some wisdom.

But certeinly, er he cam fully there,   995
But indeed, before he quite reached there,

Vanysshed was this daunce, he nyste where.
The dance had vanished, he knew not where.

No creature saugh he that bar lyf,
He saw no living creature,

Save on the grene he saugh sittynge a wyf—
Except a woman sitting on the grass—

A fouler wight ther may no man devyse.
An uglier person no man can imagine.

Agayn the knyght this olde wyf gan ryse,   1000
To meet the knight this old woman stood up

And seyde, "Sire knyght, heer forth ne lith no wey.
And said, "Sir knight, from here there is no road.

Tel me what ye seken, by youre fey!
Tell me what you seek, by your faith!

Paraventure it may the bettre be;
Perhaps it may be better for you;

Thise olde folk kan muchel thyng," quod she.
These old folk know many things," said she.

"My leeve moder," quod this knyght, "certeyn,   1005
"My dear mother," said the knight, "Certainly,

I nam but deed, but if that I kan seyn
I am but dead, unless I can say

What thyng it is that wommen moost desire.
What thing it is that women most desire.

Koude ye me wisse, I wolde wel quite youre hire."
If you could tell me, I would reward you."

"Plight me thy trouthe here in myn hand," quod she,
"Pledge me your promise here by my hand," said she,

"The nexte thyng that I requere thee,   1010
"That the next thing I require you,

Thou shalt it do, if it lye in thy myght,
You will do it, if it lies in your power,

And I wol telle it yow er it be nyght."
And I will tell it to you before night."

Goblet

1010. The promise given, with complete ignorance as to its consequences, is a favorite theme in folk literature. The audience knows at once that the promise's fulfillment will be ironic or tragic.

THE WIFE OF BATH

[Lines 1013-1035]

know the answer to the fatal question until the last possible moment. When it is revealed and the knight is saved, he is pitched immediately into his second dilemma by the old woman's demand of marriage: we go from one crisis to the next with almost melodramatic suddenness.

Chaucer's version has its moral implications. The knight begins as a brutal and selfish individual; his attitude, if not brutal, is still selfish when the old woman demands her right; but finally, when he bows to her will and gives her her choice he has made some kind of moral progression.

The happiness that comes to him at the tale's end is a reward for moral growth, and the moral lesson he learns is taught in the form of the sermon on "gentillesse." It is interesting to note that none of the folk versions of the story contain this sermon. It is Chaucer's own, deliberate addition.

"Have here my trouthe," quod the knyght, "I grante."
"Take here my pledge," said the knight, "I grant it."

"Thanne," quod she, "I dar me wel avante
"Then," said she, "I dare confidently boast

Thy lyfe is sauf; for I wol stonde therby,   1015
Your life is safe, for I can guarantee,

Upon my lyf, the queene wol seye as I.
Upon my life, the queen will agree with me.

Lat see which is the proudeste of hem alle
Let us see if the proudest of them all

That wereth on a coverchief or a calle
That wear coverchiefs or headdress

That dar seye nay of that I shal thee teche.
Will dare say no to what I teach you.

Lat us go forth withouten lenger speche."   1020
Let us go forth without further speech."

Tho rowned she a pistel in his ere,
Then she whispered a message in his ear,

And bad hym to be glad and have no fere.
And told him to be glad, and have no fear.

Whan they be comen to the court, this knyght
When they came to the court, this knight

Seyde he had holde his day, as he had hight,
Said he had kept to his day, as he had promised,

And redy was his answere, as he sayde.   1025
And had his answer ready, as he had said.

Ful many a noble wyf, and many a mayde,
Many a noble wife, and many a maid,

And many a wydwe, for that they been wise,
And many a widow, for they are wise,

The queene hirself sittyng as justise,
The queen herself sitting as judge,

Assembled been, his answere for to heere;
Were assembled, to hear his answer;

And afterward this knyght was bode appeere.   1030
And then this knight was ordered to appear.

To every wight comanded was silence,
Everyone was commanded to be silent,

And that the knyght sholde telle in audience
And the knight was ordered to tell the assembly

What thyng that worldly wommen loven best.
What thing the women of this world loved best.

This knyght ne stood nat stille as doth a best,
The knight did not stand dumb as does a beast,

But to his questioun anon answerde   1035
But answered his question at once

Pendant

THE WIFE OF BATH

[Lines 1036-1059]

With manly voys, that al the court it herde:
With manly voice, so that all the court heard it:

"My lige lady, generally," quod he,
"My liege lady, in general," said he,

"Wommen desiren to have sovereyntee
"Women desire to have authority

As wel over hir housbond as hir love,
Over their husbands as well as their lovers,

And for to been in maistrie hym above.   1040
And to be masters of them.

This is youre mooste desir, thogh ye me kille.
This is your greatest desire, though you execute me.

Dooth as yow list; I am here at youre wille."
Do as you please, I am here at your will."

In al the court ne was ther wyf, ne mayde,
In all the court there was neither wife, nor maid,

Ne wydwe, that contraried that he sayde,
Nor widow, that contradicted what he said,

But seyden he was worthy han his lyf.   1045
But said that he deserved to have his life.

And with that word up stirte the olde wyf,
And with that word up started the old woman,

Which that the knyght saugh sittyng on the grene;
Who the knight had seen sitting on the grass;

"Mercy," quod she, "my sovereyn lady queene!
"Thank you," she said, "my sovereign lady queen!

Er that youre court departe, do me right.
Before your court departs, do me justice.

I taughte this answere unto the knyght;   1050
I taught this answer to the knight,

For which he plighte me his trouhte there,
For which he pledged me his honor,

The firste thyng that I wolde hym requere
The first thing I would require of him

He wolde it do, if it lay in his myght.
He would do it, if it lay in his power.

Bifore the court thanne preye I thee, sir knyght,"
Before the court then I ask you, sir knight,"

Quod she, "that thou me take unto thy wyf;   1055
She said, "that you make me your wife;

For wel thou woost that I have kept thy lyf.
For you well know that I have saved your life.

If I seye fals, sey nay, upon thy fey!"
If I speak falsely, refuse me, on your faith!"

This knyght answerde, "Allas and weylawey!
This knight answered, "Alas and woe is me!

I woot right wel that swich was my biheste.
I know very well that such was my promise.

1039. "as hir love": according to the creed of courtly love (see Commentary), the lady ruled her lover completely, and he was totally dedicated to her service. This ideal state of affairs, the knight says, is what women want in marriage.

Helmet

Clasp

For Goddes love, as chees a newe requeste!   1060
For God's love, choose a new request!

Taak al my good and lat my body go."
Take all my property and let my body go."

"Nay thanne," quod she, "I shrewe us bothe two!
"Oh no," she said, "I curse us both!

For thogh that I be foul and oold and poore,
For though I be ugly and old and poor,

I nolde for al the metal ne for oore
I would not have all the metal or ore

That under erthe is grave or lith above,   1065
That is buried in the earth or lies above,

But if thy wyf I were and eek thy love."
Unless I were your wife and your love too."

"My love?" quod he, "nay, my dampnacion!
"My love?" said he, "no, my damnation!

Allas, that any of my nacion
Alas, that any of my birth

Sholde evere so foule disparaged be!"
Should ever be so foully dishonored!"

But al for noght; the ende is this, that he   1070
But all for nothing, the end is this, that he

Constreyned was, he nedes moste hire wedde,
Was compelled, he had to marry her,

And taketh his olde wyf, and goth to bedde.
And take his ancient wife, and go to bed.

Now wolden som men seye, paraventure,
Now some men might possibly say,

That for my necligence I do no cure
That out of negligence I take no care

To tellen yow the joye and al th'array   1075
To tell you of the joy and the festivities

That at the feste was that ilke day.
Which took place at the feast on that same day.

To which thyng shortly answeren I shal:
To which point I shall answer shortly:

I seye ther nas no joye ne feste at al;
I say there was no joy nor feast at all;

Ther nas but hevynesse and muche sorwe.
There was nothing but heaviness and much sorrow.

For prively he wedded hire on morwe,   1080
For he married her privately in the morning,

And al day after hidde hym as an owle,
And the rest of the day hid himself like an owl,

So wo was hym, his wyf looked so foule.
So woeful was he, his wife looked so foul.

Greet was the wo the knyght hadde in his thoght,
Great was the grief the knight had in his thought,

Mercury

Whan he was with his wyf abedde ybroght;
When he was brought to bed with his wife;

He walweth and he turneth to and fro.   1085
He tossed and turned to and fro.

His olde wyf lay smylyng everemo,
His old wife lay smiling all the time,

And seyde, "O deere housbonde, *benedicitee!*
And said, "O dear husband, benedicitee!

Fareth every knyght thus with his wyf as ye?
Does every knight behave with his wife as you do?

Is this the lawe of kyng Arthures hous?
Is this the custom at King Arthur's court?

Is every knyght of his so dangerous?   1090
Is every knight of his so standoffish?

I am youre owene love and eek youre wyf;
I am your own love and also your wife;

I am she which that saved hath youre lyf;
I am she who has saved your life;

And, certes, yet dide I yow nevere unright;
And truly, I have never done you wrong;

Why fare ye thus with me this firste nyght?
Why do you act this way with me this first night?

Ye faren lyk a man had lost his wit.   1095
You act like a man who has lost his wits.

What is my gilt? For Goddes love, tel it,
What is my guilt? For God's love, tell it,

And it shal been amended if I may."
And it shall be remedied if I can."

"Amended?" quod this knyght, "allas! nay, nay!
"Remedied?" said this knight, "Alas! no, no!

It wol nat been amended nevere mo.
It can never be remedied.

Thou art so loothly, and so old also,   1100
You are so loathesome, and so old as well,

And therto comen of so lowe a kynde,
And also come from such low lineage,

That litel wonder is thogh I walwe and wynde.
That it is little wonder that I toss and turn.

So wolde God myn herte wolde breste!"
Would God my heart would break!"

"Is this," quod she, "the cause of youre unreste?"
"Is this," said she, "the cause of your unrest?"

"Ye, certainly," quod he, "no wonder is."   1105
"Yes, certainly," said he, "it is no wonder."

"Now, sire," quod she, "I koude amende al this,
"Now, sir," said she, "I could remedy all this,

If that me liste, er it were dayes thre,
If I wished to, within three days,

Lady at Rabbit Warren

THE WIFE OF BATH

[Lines 1108-1131]

Some commentators have felt that the Wife of Bath's Prologue and her tale do not fit easily together, and that the boisterous, earthy character of the prologue would not have produced a story with a mythical Arthurian setting and would certainly not have included the moralizing talk on the virtues of "gentillesse."

The Chaucerian scholar R. K. Root has replied to these criticisms: "I conceive of the Wife of Bath as endowed originally with strong passions and vivid imagination, with what we are wont to call the poetic temperament. Had she been born in a palace, she might have become your typical heroine of romance, her inevitable lapses from virtue gilded over with the romantic adornments of moonlight serenades and romantic trysts. But born an heiress to a weaver's bench, there was no chance for her poetic imaginativeness to develop. Laughed at by others for her fine-spun fancies, she would certainly grow ashamed of them herself. I can believe that her excessive coarseness of speech was originally an affectation assumed to conceal the natural fineness of her nature, an affectation which easily became a second nature to her. Her strong passions demanded expression; and denied a more poetic gratification, and quite unrestrained by moral character, they express themselves in coarse vulgarity. It is only when called upon to tell a story, to leave the practical everyday world, in which she is forced to live, for the other world of fantasy, that the original imaginativeness of her nature finds opportunity to reveal itself" (The Poetry of Chaucer).

This is a gallant defense, and while it may seem a trifle far-fetched to say that the Wife's "coarseness" was originally a device to conceal the "fineness" of her nature, it is also true that the tale she tells does seem appropriate to her character in many ways. Here we can only discuss two of them.

In the first place, the lengthy analysis of "gentillesse" which the old woman gives to the knight is, in one sense, a piece of social criticism which would come quite naturally to someone in the Wife's position.

So wel ye myghte bere yow unto me.
If you behave well to me.

But, for ye speken of swich gentillesse
But as to your talk of such nobility

As is descended out of old richesse,   1110
As is descended from ancient riches,

That therfore sholden ye be gentil men,
Because of which you are noblemen,

Swich arrogance is nat worth an hen.
Such arrogance is not worth a hen.

Looke who that is moost vertuous alway,
Look at the one who is always most virtuous,

Pryvee and apert, and moost entendeth ay
Secretly and openly, and is always most concerned

To do the gentil dedes that he kan;   1115
To date whatever noble deeds he can;

Taak hym for the grettest gentil man.
Take him for the greatest nobleman.

Crist wole we clayme of hym oure gentillesse,
Christ wills we claim our nobility from him,

Nat of oure eldres for hir old richesse.
Not from our ancestors on account of their wealth.

For thogh they yeve us al hir heritage,
For though they give us all their heritage,

For which we clayme to been of heigh parage,   1120
Wherefore we claim to be of high lineage,

Yet may they nat biquethe, for no thyng,
Yet they cannot bequeath, by any means,

To noon of us hir vertuous lyvyng
To any of us their virtuous manner of living

That made hem gentil men ycalled be,
Which made them be called noblemen,

And bad us folwen hem in swich degree.
And encouraged us to follow the same pattern.

Wel kan the wise poete of Florence,   1125
Well can the wise poet of Florence,

That highte Dant, speken in this sentence.
Called Dante, speak on this theme.

Lo, in swich maner rym is Dantes tale:
Here, in this kind of rhyme is Dante's discourse:

'Ful selde up riseth by his branches smale
'Seldom rises by his own little branches

Prowesse of man, for God, of his goodnesse,
The worth of man, for God, in his goodness,

Wol that of hym we clayme oure gentilesse';   1130
Wills that from him we derive our nobility';

For of oure eldres may we no thyng clayme
From our ancestors we can derive nothing

1109. The sermon on "gentillesse" begins here. The ideas included in it were common in the Middle Ages, and Chaucer draws on Boethius, the Roman de la Rose, and Dante's Convivio.

The Richenau Crosier

1128-30. The quotation is from Dante's Purgatorio, and Chaucer has given it a somewhat compressed form. The thought is simply that man does not rise by his own virtues, but by God's.

64

THE WIFE OF BATH

[Lines 1132-1155]

Medieval society was hierarchical, based on the relationship of the landowning lord to the peasant-tenant. The privilege of birthright was very strong and with it the assumption that society was naturally divided into aristocrat and serf.

During the Middle Ages this hierarchy was disturbed by the growth of a new class, the burghers or merchants (now bourgeoisie), to which the Wife belonged. This new mercantile class was not readily accepted by the traditional aristocrats; people in the Wife's position would be made aware, on many occasions, of their low origins and lack of privilege, whether they had material wealth (as the Wife had) or not.

Thus the "gentillesse" passage, which argues that real nobility, or virtue, has nothing to do with inherited social rank represents what might very well be the Wife's point of view.

It should also be added that Chaucer, who was a court official and saw much of the nobility without being one of their number, would probably take the same view. However, he would be wise enough not to express it directly, and the Wife may have provided a convenient mask.

In the second place there are things in the Wife's tale that remind us forcefully of her situation at the end of the prologue. There she is left with the memory of her five husbands, a woman who has once been "lusty" and attractive, and is now slipping, resentfully, into middle age. She may hope for another husband—"Welcome the sixte whan that evere he shal!"—but we are not sure she will get him.

What could come more naturally, as a fantasy of wish-fulfillment, than a story of an old woman miraculously restored to youth, beauty, and a young husband? As with most of the pilgrims' stories, the Wife's tale is not only of interest in itself, it is also an astute comment on the person who tells it.

On a purely didactic level the tale is, of course, meant to bear out the thesis proposed by the

But temporel thyng that man may hurte and mayme.
But temporal things that man may hurt and injure.

Eek every wight woot this as wel as I,
Besides everyone knows this as well as I,

If gentillesse were planted naturelly
If nobility were implanted by nature

Unto a certeyn lynage doun the lyne,   1135
To a certain lineage, down the line,

Pryvee and apert, thanne wolde they nevere fyne
Then secretly and openly they would never cease

To doon of gentillesse the faire office;
To do the good deeds of nobility;

They myghte do no vileynye or vice.
They could not commit any sin or evil.

Taak fyr, and bere it in the derkeste hous
Take fire, and carry it to the darkest house

Bitwix this and the mount of Kaukasous,   1140
Between here and the mount of Caucasus,

And lat men shette the dores and go thenne;
And let men shut the doors and go away;

Yet wol the fyr as faire lye and brenne
Yet the fire will as brightly blaze and burn

As twenty thousand men myghte it biholde;
As if twenty thousand men were watching it;

His office naturel ay wol it holde,
It will keep to its natural function,

Up peril of my lyf, til that it dye.   1145
On peril of my life, until it dies.

Here may ye se wel how that genterye
Here you can well see that gentility

Is nat annexed to possession,
Is not connected to possession,

Sith folk ne doon hir operacion
Since folk do not behave

Alwey, as dooth the fyr, lo, in his kynde.
Always, as the fire does, according to its nature.

For, God it woot, men may wel often fynde   1150
For, God knows, men may often find

A lordes sone do shame and vileynye.
A lord's son doing things shameful and low.

And he that wol han pris of his gentrye,
And he who would have his rank esteemed

For he was boren of a gentil hous,
Because he was born of a noble house,

And hadde his eldres noble and vertuous,
And had noble and virtuous ancestors,

And nyl hymselven do no gentil dedis,   1155
And will not himself do noble deeds,

1148-49. i.e., the property of burning is natural to fire in any situation; but the so-called nobility do not naturally possess "gentilesse" in the same way.

THE WIFE OF BATH

[Lines 1156-1179]

Wife in her prologue: marriage is happy when the wife is dominant. Just as Jenkin, by succumbing to the Wife, wins peace for both of them, so the knight, by giving way to his wife, rejuvenates her and insures his own happiness.

Secure in the rightness of her argument the Wife, at the end of the tale, reverts to the sentiments of the prologue, damning the "olde and angry" and rejoicing in the "yonge, and fressh abedde."

Ring

Ne folwen his gentil auncestre that deed is,
Nor follow the example of his noble ancestor that is dead,

He nys nat gentil, be he duc or erl;
He is not noble, be he duke or earl;

For vileyns synful dedes make a cherl.
For low sinful deeds make a base man.

For gentillesse nys but renomee
For nobleness is not only the renown

Of thyne auncestres, for hir heigh bountee,   1160
Of your ancestors, because of their excellence,

Which is a strange thyng to thy persone.
Which is not inherent in yourself.

Thy gentillesse cometh fro God allone.
Your nobility comes from God alone.

Thanne comth oure verray gentillesse of grace;
So our true nobility comes through grace;

It was no thyng biquethe us with oure place.
It is not bequeathed to us with our rank.

Thenketh how noble, as seith Valerius,   1165
Think how noble, as Valerius says,

Was thilke Tullius Hostillius,
Was that Tullus Hostilius,

That out of poverte roos to heigh noblesse.
Who from poverty rose to high nobility.

Redeth Senek, and redeth eek Boece;
Read Seneca, and read Boethius too;

Ther shul ye seen expres that it no drede is
There shall you clearly see that there is no doubt

That he is gentil that dooth gentil dedis.   1170
That he is noble that does noble deeds.

And therfore, leeve housbonde, I thus conclude:
And therefore, dear husband, I thus conclude:

Al were it that myne auncestres were rude,
Although it may be my ancestors were lowborn,

Yet may the hye God, and so hope I,
Yet may the high God, and so I hope,

Grante me grace to lyven vertuously.
Grant me the grace to live virtuously.

Thanne am I gentil, whan that I bigynne   1175
Then am I noble, when I begin

To lyven vertuously and weyve synne.
To live virtuously and avoid sin.

And ther as ye of poverte me repreeve,
And whereas you reprove me for poverty,

The hye God on whom that we bileeve,
The high God in whom we believe,

In wilful poverte chees to lyve his lyf.
Chose poverty in which to live his life.

1165. Valerius Maximus was a Roman historian in the time of the Emperor Tiberius, in one of whose works, illustrating the moral virtues, the story of Tullus Hostilius appears.

1166. Tullus Hostilius, who began as a herdsman, rose to become a King of Rome.

1168. Seneca and Boethius, Roman philosophers.

Shoe.

66

And certes every man, mayden, or wyf,   1180
And certainly every man, maid, or wife,

May understonde that Jhesus, hevene kyng,
Can understand that Jesus, heaven's king,

Ne wolde nat chese a vicious lyvyng.
Would not choose an evil way of living.

Glad poverte is an honest thyng, certeyn;
Cheerful poverty is an honest thing, to be sure;

This wol Senec and othere clerkes seyn.
This will Seneca and other clerks all say.

Whoso that halt hym payd of his poverte,   1185
Whoever is contented in his poverty,

I holde hym riche, al hadde he nat a sherte.
I consider him rich, even if he has no shirt.

He that coveiteth is a povre wight,
He who covets is a poor person,

For he wolde han that is nat in his myght;
For he would have what is not in his power;

But he that noght hath, ne coveiteth have
But he that has nothing, and wants nothing,

Is riche, although ye holde hym but a knave.   1190
Is rich, although you consider him only a peasant.

Verray poverte, it syngeth proprely;
True poverty sings by nature;

Music and Courtship

Juvenal seith of poverte myrily:
Juvenal says merrily of poverty:

'The povre man, whan he goth by the weye,
'The poor man, when he walks on his way,

Bifore the theves he may synge and pleye.'
In the presence of thieves may sing and play.'

Poverte is hateful good and, as I gesse,   1195
Poverty is unpleasant yet good, and, I imagine,

A ful greet bryngere out of bisynesse;
A great bringer out of industry;

A greet amendere eek of sapience
A great improver also of wisdom

To hym that taketh it in pacience.
To him that accepts it with patience.

Poverte is this, although it seme alenge,
Poverty is this, although it may seem miserable,

Possession that no wight wol chalenge.   1200
A possession no man will challenge.

Poverte ful ofte, whan a man is lowe,
Poverty very often, when a man is brought low,

Maketh his God and eek hymself to knowe.
Makes him know his God and himself as well.

Poverte a spectacle is, as thynketh me,
Poverty is an eyeglass, it seems to me,

Thurgh which he may his verray freendes see.
Through which one may see his real friends.

And therfore, sire, syn that I noght yow greve,   1205
And therefore, sir, since I do not harm you,

Of my poverte namoore ye me repreve.
By my poverty, reprove me no more.

Now, sire, of elde ye repreve me;
Now, sir, you reprove me with age;

And certes, sire, thogh noon auctoritee
And truly, sir, though no authority

Were in no book, ye gentils of honour
Were in any book, you honorable gentlemen

Seyn that men sholde an old wight doon favour,   1210
Say that men should be courteous to an old person,

And clepe hym fader, for youre gentillesse;
And call him father, out of your gentility;

And auctours shal I fynden, as I gesse.
And I could find authorities for that, I imagine.

Now ther ye seye that I am foul and old,
Now when you say that I am foul and old,

Than drede you noght to been a cokewold;
Then you need have no fear of being made a cuckold;

For filthe and eelde, also moot I thee,   1215
For filth and old age, I can tell you,

Servingmen of Chaucer's Time

Been grete wardeyns upon chastitee.
Are great guardians of chastity.

But nathelees, syn I knowe youre delit,
But nevertheless, since I know your pleasure,

I shal fulfille youre worldly appetit.
I shall fulfill your worldly appetite."

Chese now," quod she, "oon of thise thynges tweye:
"Choose now," said she, "one of these two things:

To han me foul and old til that I deye,   1220
To have me foul and old until I die,

And be to yow a trewe, humble wyf,
And be to you a faithful, humble wife,

And nevere yow displese in al my lyf;
And never displease you in my whole life;

Or elles ye wol han me yong and fair,
Or else to have me young and fair,

And take youre aventure of the repair
And take your chance on the visitors

That shal be to youre hous by cause of me,   1225
Who come to your house because of me,

Or in som oother place, may wel be.
Or meet me somewhere else, it may well be.

Now chese yourselven wheither that yow liketh."
Now choose yourself whichever pleases you."

This knyght avyseth hym and sore siketh,
The knight considered and sighed painfully,

But atte laste he seyde in this manere:
But at last he spoke in this manner:

"My lady and my love, and wyf so deere,   1230
"My lady and my love, and wife so dear,

I put me in youre wise governance;
I put myself under your authority;

Cheseth youreself which may be moost plesance
Choose yourself whichever may bring most pleasure

And moost honour to yow and me also.
And most honor to you as well as me.

I do no fors the wheither of the two;
I make no choice between the two;

For as yow liketh, it suffiseth me."   1235
For what pleases you suffices me."

"Thanne have I gete of yow maistrie," quod she,
"Then I have mastery over you," she said,

"Syn I may chese and governe as me lest?"
"Since I may choose and govern as I like?"

"Ye, certes, wyf," quod he, "I holde it best."
"Yes, certainly, wife," said he, "I think it best."

"Kys me," quod she, "we be no lenger wrothe;
"Kiss me," said she, "we are no longer angry;

For, by my trouthe, I wol be to yow bothe,   1240
For, by my faith, I will be both to you,

This is to seyn, ye, bothe fair and good.
Which is to say, yes, both fair and good.

I prey to God that I moote sterven wood,
I pray to God that I may die mad,

But I to yow be also good and trewe
Unless I am as good and faithful to you

As evere was wyf syn that the world was newe.
As ever wife was since the world was new.

And but I be to-morn as fair to seene   1245
And unless I be in the morning as fair to see

As any lady, emperice, or queene,
As any lady, empress, or queen,

That is bitwixe the est and eek the west,
That lives between the east and the west,

Do with my lyf and deth right as yow lest.
Decide my life and death however you please.

Cast up the curtyn, looke how that it is."
Open the curtain, see how it is."

And whan the knyght saugh verraily al this,   1250
And when the knight truly saw all this,

Effigy of a Lady

THE WIFE OF BATH

[Lines 1251-1264]

That she so fair was, and so yong therto,
That she was so fair, and so young as well,

For joye he hente hire in his armes two,
For joy he seized her in his two arms,

His herte bathed in a bath of blisse.
His heart bathed in a bath of bliss.

A thousand tyme a-rewe he gan hir kisse,
A thousand times in succession he kissed her,

And she obeyed hym in every thyng   1255
And she obeyed him in everything

That myghte do hym plesance or likyng.
That might give him pleasure or delight.

And thus they lyve unto hir lyves ende
And so they lived to the end of their lives

In parfit joye; and Jhesu Crist us sende
In perfect joy; and may Jesus Christ send us

Housbondes meeke, yonge, and fressh abedde,
Husbands obedient, young, and fresh in bed,

And grace t' overbyde hem that we wedde;   1260
And the grace to outlive those we wed;

And eek I praye Jhesu shorte hir lyves
And I also pray Jesus to shorten their lives

That wol nat be governed by hir wyves;
Who will not be governed by their wives;

And olde and angry nygardes of dispence,
And for old and angry misers in spending,

God sende hem soone verray pestilence!
God send them soon the plague itself!

Heere endeth the Wyves Tale of Bathe.
Here ends the Wife of Bath's Tale

70

NOTES

NOTES